NEEDS ASSESSMENT

NEEDS ASSESSMENT

PHASE III
Taking Action for Change

Laurie Stevahn
Seattle University

Jean A. King
University of Minnesota

Series Editor: James W. Altschuld

NEEDS ASSESSMENT KIT **5**

SSAGE

Los Angeles | London | New Delhi
Singapore | Washington DC

For information:

SAGE Publications, Inc.
2455 Teller Road
Thousand Oaks,
  California 91320
E-mail: order@sagepub.com

SAGE Publications India Pvt. Ltd.
B 1/I 1 Mohan Cooperative
  Industrial Area
Mathura Road, New Delhi 110 044
India

SAGE Publications Ltd.
1 Oliver's Yard
55 City Road
London EC1Y 1SP
United Kingdom

SAGE Publications
  Asia-Pacific Pte. Ltd.
33 Pekin Street #02-01
Far East Square
Singapore 048763

Printed in the United States of America

Library of Congress Cataloging-in-Publication Data

Stevahn, Laurie.
Needs assessment Phase III: taking action for change (book 5)/Laurie Stevahn, Jean A. King.
    p. cm.
Includes bibliographical references and index.
ISBN 978-1-4129-7583-4 (pbk.)
  1. Strategic planning. 2. Needs assessment. 3. Organizational change. 4. Needs assessment—Evaluation. I. King, Jean A. II. Title.

HD30.28.A38855 2010
658.4′012—dc22   2009027655

This book is printed on acid-free paper.

09 10 11 12 13   10 9 8 7 6 5 4 3 2 1

Acquisitions Editor:	Vicki Knight
Associate Editor:	Lauren Habib
Editorial Assistant:	Ashley Dodd
Production Editor:	Brittany Bauhaus
Copy Editor:	Melinda Masson
Typesetter:	C&M Digitals (P) Ltd.
Proofreader:	Victoria Reed-Castro
Indexer:	Diggs Publication Services, Inc.
Cover Designer:	Candice Harman
Marketing Manager:	Stephanie Adams

Brief Contents

Detailed Contents

Preface

The real voyage of discovery consists not in seeking new landscapes but in having new eyes.

—Marcel Proust
French Novelist (1871–1922)

Previous volumes in this Needs Assessment KIT have laid the foundation for successfully conducting needs assessment studies by outlining three phases in the process: (a) preassessment, (b) needs assessment, and (c) postassessment. The first four books provide concrete steps for carrying out the first two phases. This volume focuses on the third phase by describing how to create and implement an action plan derived from needs priorities in ways that will enhance organizational learning and support future success.

Ultimately, people will judge the success of any needs assessment by the extent to which it enables their organization to change, develop, and learn to better achieve its purposes. Like embarking on a family voyage to a targeted destination, conducting a needs assessment requires that people get on board and interact constructively for the journey to be successful. Because effective change within any organization is a collaborative journey, we use the metaphor of travel to present steps in the postassessment phase of needs assessment studies.

Chapter 1 briefly revisits the three-phase model of needs assessment presented throughout this KIT and challenges evaluators to take the road less traveled by fully pursuing postassessment. This primarily entails developing and implementing an action plan for meaningful change.

Chapter 2 describes aspects of blazing the trail when transitioning from needs assessment to postassessment. This involves attending to the nuts and bolts of preplanning, for which we offer practical suggestions and adaptable templates.

Chapter 3 presents strategies for collaborating to create and implement the action plan. Here we present a double dozen facilitation procedures useful for promoting positive relations, developing shared understandings, prioritizing and finalizing decisions, and assessing progress.

Chapter 4 focuses on weathering the storms of interpersonal conflict that inevitably surface in any change effort. Frameworks and competencies for constructive conflict resolution can help needs assessors negotiate these challenging terrains.

Chapter 5 cautions against unforeseen individual and organizational roadblocks that challenge change efforts. Expecting the unexpected in advance and considering an array of helpful responses can keep postassessment efforts on track.

Chapter 6 outlines important considerations when formally evaluating the entire expedition and documenting conclusions for future use. Planning formative, summative, and reflective evaluation activities at the onset helps ensure that this step in postassessment actually takes place.

The Epilogue briefly recaps the postassessment journey. Here we share final words of wisdom, highlighting how skillful practitioners artfully apply the science of needs assessment to conduct successful studies.

Distinctive features of this volume include

- a postassessment map that succinctly outlines purposes, steps, decisions, and questions to guide the entire process;
- templates adaptable across needs assessment contexts for creating meeting agendas, reflection feedback sheets, "to do" lists, action plans, timetables, and working norms;
- a double dozen facilitation procedures with directions and sample materials for collaboratively developing, implementing, and assessing the needs assessment action plan;
- practical frameworks and step-by-step strategies for managing interpersonal conflict constructively;
- concrete ideas for responding to unexpected individual characteristics and organizational issues that can block successful change efforts; and
- templates for planning how to evaluate the entire needs assessment from the onset.

Anyone doing needs assessment work will find these features useful, especially needs assessors and organizational or program leaders guiding the process. Others, however, will also benefit from the ideas and materials contained in this volume. For example, instructors who teach needs assessment or program evaluation in universities or professional development settings can use this book as a resource. Students can use the tools in this book to illustrate theoretical concepts or to carry out internship practicums. Program administrators will find this a concise desktop reference to assist in getting the results of evaluations used. Consultants specializing in program evaluation, group facilitation, or organization development also can apply the frameworks and templates in this book across a wide range of contexts, such as in social work, health, education, social services, business, government, nonprofits, foundations, and so on. Whatever your role and wherever your landscapes, we hope that you make the materials in this volume your own.

Acknowledgments

We are indeed grateful for opportunities to work together on evaluation projects, including the writing of this volume. As collaborators, we relish the challenge and privilege of living the ideas presented in this book as we continue to learn from and with each other. Our ongoing professional partnership has only deepened our commitment to cooperative processes and the power of constructive participatory endeavors. We especially thank Jim Altschuld, editor of this Needs Assessment KIT, for inviting us to join his team. We also heartily thank those in our respective circles who sustain us in wonderful ways. Laurie thanks her family, friends, and communities of faith who nourish her soul and colleagues near and far whose warmth, encouragement, and mutual grappling enhance the joy of inquiry. Jean thanks her husband Stuart Appelbaum for his enduring support, keen wit, sense of fun, and editorial expertise and her student and community collaborators who continue to provide new lessons, examples, and inspiration. We sincerely thank those at SAGE who have dedicated time and talent to this volume, especially Vicki Knight, acquisitions editor, for providing thoughtful and insightful guidance, and the entire editorial, production, and marketing team for attending to every detail. Finally, we and SAGE gratefully acknowledge the contributions of the following reviewers who took time during a busy academic year to provide helpful feedback:

Ellen Darden, *Concord University*

Lizanne DeStefano, *University of Illinois*

Doug Leigh, *Pepperdine University*

Wendy Lewandowski, *Kent State University*

Kui-Hee Song, *California State University, Chico*

Ryan Watkins, *George Washington University*

About the Authors

Laurie Stevahn, PhD, is associate professor in the College of Education at Seattle University where she teaches graduate courses in educational research, social justice in professional practice, models of teaching and assessment for learning, and leadership for effective schools. She earned her doctorate in educational psychology from the University of Minnesota, her master's in curriculum and instruction from Seattle Pacific University, and her bachelor's in political science from Pacific Lutheran University. Prior to joining the academy, she taught high school social studies and mathematics in Washington state and founded Professional Development Associates, her consulting company specializing in human resource and organization development, program design and implementation, and participatory evaluation for capacity building. Laurie conducts research on conflict resolution training and essential competencies for program evaluators and has published on these topics in a variety of journals including the *American Educational Research Journal*, *American Journal of Evaluation*, *Child Development*, and others. She also is coauthor of two books for educators, *Cooperative Learning: Where Heart Meets Mind* and *The Portfolio Organizer: Succeeding With Portfolios in Your Classroom*. Honors include the National Staff Development Council's Best Non-Dissertation Research Award for examining the effectiveness of the Louisiana Center for Law and Civic Education's teen leadership program on conflict resolution and violence prevention. She is past chair of two American Educational Research Association Special Interest Groups (Cooperative Learning: Theory, Research, and Practice; Conflict Resolution and Violence Prevention) and currently serves on the International Association for the Study of Cooperation in Education executive board of directors. In addition to her work with organizations across the United States, Laurie's international work includes invited presentations in Australia, Canada, the Czech Republic, Greece, Italy, and the Netherlands.

Jean A. King, PhD, is professor in the Department of Organizational Leadership, Policy, and Development at the University of Minnesota where she teaches and coordinates the evaluation studies graduate and certificate programs and the all-university program evaluation minor. She received her bachelor's, master's, and doctoral degrees from Cornell University and taught middle school English in upstate New York before moving to a faculty position at Tulane University in New Orleans, Louisiana. In 1989 she moved upriver to the University of Minnesota as the founding director of the Center for Applied Research and Educational Improvement in the College of Education and Human Development, a position she held for 4 years before working collaboratively to revitalize program evaluation instruction in the college. In 1996 she created the Minnesota Evaluation Studies Institute, an annual forum for local and national evaluators. Jean has received numerous awards for her work, including the Myrdahl Award for Evaluation Practice and the Robert Ingle Award for Extraordinary Service from the American Evaluation Association; three teaching awards (the University of Minnesota's Award for Outstanding Contributions to Post-baccalaureate, Graduate, and Professional Education, and the College of Education and Human Development's Distinguished Teaching Award and Robert H. Beck Faculty Teaching Award for Outstanding Instruction); and three community service awards. A sought-after presenter and long-time writer on evaluation topics, she is the author of numerous articles, chapters, and reviews and has an abiding interest in participatory evaluation and evaluation capacity building.

1

Postassessment

Mapping the Road Less Traveled

Two roads diverged in a wood, and I—I took the one less traveled by,
And that has made all the difference.

—Robert Frost, "The Road Not Taken"
American Poet (1874–1963)

❖ INTRODUCTION

On any expedition, taking a road less traveled presents both risk and opportunity. The risk entails entering unknown territory that may require exceptional energy, courage, ingenuity, and perseverance. The opportunity entails great potential for positive impact, which, if realized, will make all the difference. The three-phase model of needs assessment often represents the road less traveled by systematically outlining a comprehensive set of steps for identifying needs, planning for change, and monitoring progress (see Altschuld & Kumar, 2009; Altschuld & Witkin, 1999). The road more traveled tends to be one in which people launch a survey, confuse needs with solutions, and then make quick inferences about how to deal with concerns rather than thoroughly measuring or mapping discrepancies between "what is" (existing conditions) and "what should be" (desired conditions). Such haste leads to piecemeal approaches to assessment that often fall short of well-intended purposes.

This volume will assist needs assessors in taking the full journey by enacting the third phase, which entails translating solution strategies derived from identified needs into needs-based actions. This phase is inextricably intertwined with issues of organizational learning, continuous improvement, and effective change, none of which happen without the commitment and collaborative efforts of organizational leaders and members. This book, therefore, focuses on facilitation skills and strategies designed to involve others meaningfully in the process of change.

We begin this chapter by briefly revisiting the three-phase model of needs assessment to situate postassessment within its larger context. We then focus on what postassessment entails—its importance, requirements, and challenges. Finally, we offer several frameworks for conceptualizing and guiding postassessment, a process most fundamentally characterized by planning and implementing actions derived from identified and prioritized needs.

❖ THREE-PHASE MODEL OF NEEDS ASSESSMENT

A comprehensive needs assessment goes far beyond conducting a survey, brainstorming solutions to concerns, or focusing mainly on those within the organization who provide services to people in hopes of improving performance. Instead, a well-designed and fully implemented assessment will examine complexities across multiple phases that unfold over time and multiple levels of needs within each phase. The three-phase model of needs assessment is one paradigm that captures such complexity (see Table 1.1). The model assists needs assessors not only in envisioning the entire process from the outset but also in facilitating the types of activities that lead to success.

Since the other books in the KIT explain the model in detail, here we briefly review it by highlighting two of its essential assumptions. First, needs exist at three levels: clients, program providers, and organizational systems. Each of these levels should be considered throughout the entire process. Second, a comprehensive needs assessment consists of three distinct phases: preassessment, needs assessment, and postassessment. Although each serves a different purpose, together

Table 1.1   Three-Phase Model of Needs Assessment

Phases	Purposes	Steps
Phase I **Preassessment**	Focus and initiate the assessment Examine existing data Decide whether to proceed	1. Focus the assessment 2. Form a needs assessment committee 3. Examine existing data to determine current and desired conditions; identify discrepancies 4. Decide to stop or proceed to Phase II and/or III
Phase II **Needs Assessment**	Collect and examine additional data Develop deeper understanding of needs at Levels 1, 2, and 3 Consider causes of needs Establish initial priorities	5. Collect additional data on current and desired conditions 6. Identify discrepancies at Levels 1, 2, and 3 7. Prioritize discrepancies 8. Causally analyze needs 9. Identify solution criteria and possible solution strategies 10. Proceed to Phase III
Phase III **Postassessment**	Prioritize solution strategies derived from identified needs Create and implement an action plan Evaluate/document the assessment	11. Make final decisions on resolving needs and selecting solution strategies 12. Create and communicate an action plan; build commitment/support for the plan 13. Implement and monitor the plan 14. Evaluate and document the entire assessment for future endeavors

Source: From Altschuld, J. W., & Kumar, D. D. (2009). *Needs assessment: An overview,* p. 34. Thousand Oaks, CA: Sage.

these phases progressively guide the activities necessary for a thorough and successful endeavor.

Levels

Needs within organizations or programs may exist at three levels. The first level focuses on the needs of clients or people served. Attending to those who receive an organization's programs, products, or services is crucial because they are the reasons the organization exists in the first place. The second level focuses on the needs of service providers who work in the organization. Their lived experiences and perceived realities may directly affect their capacity to deliver programs or services to clients. The third level focuses on the needs of the organizational system. This pertains to structural systems and organizational norms that support both those who provide and those who receive program services.

For example, immigrant families who receive services in the United States from a local community food bank will have needs related to the special characteristics of their culture (Somali, Mexican, and Hmong cuisines involve different types of food), immigration status, ability to speak English, and so on. The staff who work in the food bank have different needs related to managing the clients' visits and deciding which families from which zip codes are eligible, how often families can get food, and how much they can get at each visit. At the third level the organization must address systemic needs such as how to increase the amount of food available given the growing demand in the community. All three of these levels are interdependent, each affecting the others. When Hmong clients move out of the area served by the food bank, the staff must decide if they remain eligible for food; at the same time the broader system needs to ensure that food will be available for them. This interconnection of needs at three levels explains why it is important to keep all three in mind throughout the entire assessment process.

Phases

The needs assessment model also has three phases that progress over time. Table 1.1 outlines these sequential phases, each providing a foundation for the next. The first phase, preassessment, involves initiating and focusing the effort, forming a needs assessment committee (NAC) to guide the process, examining existing data to determine needs (keeping in mind all three levels), and facilitating decision making—especially whether to stop if needs do not exist or are deemed insignificant or to proceed if more in-depth information is required to identify or better understand needs. The second phase, needs assessment, requires collecting and examining additional data, identifying and prioritizing discrepancies across all three levels of needs, considering causes underlying the identified needs, establishing solution criteria, developing solution strategies, and deciding when to proceed to the final phase. The third phase, postassessment, includes prioritizing and making final decisions about key needs, selecting solution strategies and developing an action plan, communicating and garnering support for the plan, implementing and monitoring it, and evaluating and documenting the entire process.

❖ POSTASSESSMENT

Understanding the postassessment phase begins by addressing three fundamental questions: Why is postassessment important? What does postassessment require? What special challenges are inherent in the postassessment process?

Importance

The importance of postassessment cannot be overstated because little or nothing happens without it. Information that emerges during the first two phases will likely remain just that—information—without strategically planning how to use results for effective change. Postassessment positions an organization for improvement, which is why the needs assessment was carried out in the first place. Ultimately, the cost-effectiveness of any assessment is linked to whether its results get used. Why devote precious resources, human or financial, to improvement strategies that don't get implemented? Furthermore, not using results may leave organizational members who devoted energy to the effort feeling frustrated or demoralized once they realize that nothing will come of it. Such negative unintended consequences almost certainly will tarnish morale and commitment, which can compound problematic issues that existed prior to the endeavor, making what were difficult situations even worse.

Steps in the postassessment phase particularly equip those involved to take action for positive change. These steps include finalizing prioritized needs and solution strategies, creating a plan to carry out the strategies, communicating and gaining support for the plan, implementing and monitoring activities, and evaluating and documenting the entire process to provide valuable information for future endeavors. Like pebbles dropped into a pond, these activities have the potential to initiate rippling waves that eventually permeate the organization, producing numerous benefits:

1. An enhanced sense of mission for organizational members

2. Strengthened commitment to organizational values

3. Greater ownership for and commitment to targeted outcomes

4. More cohesive collegial relations

5. Revitalized energy and productivity

6. Increased individual and organizational capacity for continuous improvement through ongoing assessment

Of course, realizing these as well as other possible benefits depends on the extent to which those facilitating postassessment attend to its requirements for success.

Requirements

First and foremost, individuals leading postassessment must understand how to orient efforts toward change. This requires comprehending factors associated with effective organizational behavior and acquiring the skills necessary to facilitate constructive action. Factors include knowledge and appreciation of the complexity of change, its process orientation, the limitations of top-down mandates, the benefits of broad involvement, the inevitability of unexpected disruptions, and the connection between collective aims and individual aspirations.

Dealing with the change factors noted above requires needs assessors to exercise a range of competencies that include acquiring conceptual knowledge about organizational change and employing interpersonal, technical, and facilitation skills to enact it. Conceptual knowledge of change provides guidance for structuring postassessment tasks in ways that will promote the effective use of needs assessment results. Interpersonal skills such as seeking input from everyone, listening to alternative viewpoints, communicating understanding, appreciating diverse life experiences, conveying respect, reaching agreement, and managing conflict constructively foster positive working relationships among diverse individuals whose collective actions ultimately will determine whether change occurs. Technical skills such as managing databases, analyzing information, developing logic models, and writing action plans provide the nuts and bolts that give concrete form to the change process. Facilitation skills keep the process in motion by structuring postassessment tasks for effective communication, collaboration, conflict management, and decision making. Collectively, these factors work together to transform results into meaningful action that embodies change.

Challenges

Perhaps the most immediate and discernible challenge in postassessment is how to skillfully apply the competencies necessary for change. Beyond that, the major challenge deals with the complexity of change itself and the unpredictable nature of circumstances outside of any one person's control. Even with a well-equipped tool kit, needs assessors cannot possibly predict the unlimited number of unexpected events that, for bad or good, will influence postassessment. For example, political, economic, or social situations change without warning; new hires join the organization weekly as demand for services skyrockets; a key organizational leader goes on sabbatical; a financial shortfall requires immediate budget cuts; a rumor fuels interpersonal conflicts among employees; the chair of the NAC is unexpectedly hospitalized; an anonymous donor funds a large endowment but with specifications that likely will divert attention away from the needs assessment; a program recipient files a lawsuit against the organization; and so on. These as well as other unforeseen incidents can easily derail efforts, necessitating skillful responses from needs assessors who must attempt to keep the postassessment process on track.

❖ GUIDING FRAMEWORKS FOR POSTASSESSMENT

Subsequent chapters offer ideas, strategies, and examples for facilitating the postassessment phase. Here we suggest two frameworks for conceptualizing and guiding that facilitation. The first is the Three-Phase Model Matrix, which considers how levels of needs (clients, program providers, and organizational systems) interface with the temporal phases of assessment (preassessment, needs assessment, and postassessment). The second is the Postassessment Map, which translates the steps characterizing this phase into key questions for decision making. Brief elaborations of each follow.

Three-Phase Model Matrix

The Three-Phase Model Matrix in Table 1.2 illustrates that three levels of needs are inherent throughout all phases of assessment. As each phase unfolds, however, the levels are differentially important. The shaded areas indicate that all levels should be taken into account throughout, while check marks indicate emphasis on particular levels within each phase.

Table 1.2   Three-Phase Model Matrix

Phases \ Levels	Level 1 Clients/Recipients	Level 2 Program Providers	Level 3 Organizational System Supports
Phase I Preassessment	✓		
Phase II Needs Assessment	✓	✓	✓
Phase III Postassessment			✓

Note: Although Level 1 needs always warrant attention because an organization or a program ultimately exists to serve its clients, a comprehensive assessment will consider all levels of needs throughout (signified by shaded areas). Certain levels, however, support purposes unique to each phase as the assessment progresses (signified by check marks). Level 3 needs become central to successful change during postassessment.

In Phase I, for example, the needs of clients take priority because an organization ultimately exists to serve its clients. Although the needs of service providers and organizational system supports should not be ignored, those of clients fundamentally focus the entire needs assessment toward improving the programs, products, or services that the organization provides.

In Phase II, equal emphasis on all three levels seems prudent given the often close connections among clients, program providers, and organizational systems. If the needs of program providers go unmet, it is less likely that they will be able to serve their clients well. Similarly, if systems needs go unmet, the programs or services that providers offer are likely to suffer from conditions that negatively affect their performance. Such less-than-optimal performance directly affects clients who end up receiving substandard services or programs.

In Phase III, attending to the needs of organizational support systems becomes especially important to successfully dealing with the needs of program providers and clients. This does not mean that the needs of clients and program providers should be disregarded; rather, the focus shifts toward strengthening organizational systems that support the implementation of an action plan designed to address the needs of those who provide services and those who receive them. Such systems include the structural foundations and social networks that define the organization (e.g., roles and responsibilities, policies and procedures, and norms and expectations for communication and interaction). Essentially, these organizational systems play a central role in change efforts by either enhancing or impeding the development and enactment of strategic plans designed to address identified needs. Needs assessors who know how to strengthen support at the systems level will be better able to promote meaningful efforts toward successful change. This book provides practical tools and strategies for doing just that—spearheading and sustaining constructive change.

Postassessment Map

The Postassessment Map in Table 1.3 more fully explicates components that comprise the third phase. Columns 1 and 2 show the purposes and steps in chronological order and how they are related. Observe that the four steps that enable needs assessors to accomplish the three purposes do not align exactly. Instead, Steps 11, 12, 13, and 14 span across the purposes of postassessment in an overlapping fashion. For example, Step 11 accomplishes the first purpose, which involves making final decisions on resolving needs and selecting solution strategies. This step also encompasses part of the second purpose of postassessment, creating and implementing an action plan. In reality, the end of Step 11 is interwoven with the initial activities in creating a plan. This leads to Step 12, creating, communicating, and building support/commitment for the plan, which constitutes the core of the second purpose of postassessment. Step 13 also spans two purposes of postassessment: Implementing the plan relates to the second purpose, whereas monitoring, documenting, and evaluating it relates to the third purpose. Step 14, evaluating and documenting the entire needs assessment for future use, completes the third and final purpose of postassessment.

The Postassessment Map also lists decisions and questions in Columns 3 and 4 to guide needs assessors through each of the steps in Column 2. Items in the third column specify major decisions that must be made in each step; items in the fourth column state the decisions as guiding questions.

Table 1.3 Postassessment Map

Purposes	Steps	Decisions	Questions
Prioritize solution strategies derived from identified needs	11. Make final decisions on resolving needs and selecting solution strategies	Determining needs-based priorities	Should we take action (at all)?
		Identifying criteria and standards	How will we know which solution strategies are the best?
		Considering alternative solution strategies	What action choices are possible?
Create and implement an action plan	12. Create and communicate an action plan; build commitment/ support for the plan	Developing the action plan	Who needs to be involved? What's the best plan of action?
		Communicating the action plan	Who needs to know? When? In what format?
		Building support for the action plan	How can we increase commitment to the action plan?
	13. Implement and monitor the plan	Implementing the action plan	What tasks must be completed to implement the action plan? Who will do them? When?
Document the implementation and evaluate the entire NA		Documenting the implementation	What are we doing? How are we keeping track of what is happening? Are people doing what they said they would?
		Monitoring the implementation	What progress are we making on the action plan?
	14. Evaluate and document the entire NA for future endeavors	Evaluating the NA (formative)	How are we doing (as the process unfolds)?
		Evaluating the NA (summative)	How did we do (once the process is completed)?
		Learning from the NA experience	What did we learn?

In other words, Step 11 directs needs assessors to facilitate decision making on whether (if at all) to take action on needs-based priorities, which criteria and standards to use in adopting the best solution strategies, and which alternative solution strategies exist for possible adoption. Step 12 points needs assessors toward seeking ways to develop an effective and feasible plan of action, to communicate it in timely and meaningful ways to those who need to know, and to build support for and commitment to the endeavor. Step 13 focuses attention on facilitating tasks and timelines necessary for implementing the action plan, documenting and tracking the tasks as they are completed, and monitoring overall progress. Finally, Step 14 positions needs assessors to evaluate efforts as the process unfolds (formative), to evaluate the entire assessment at its completion (summative), and to determine what was learned from the experience.

Although elements in the Postassessment Map appear as distinct items in chronological order, they tend to merge into each other. Step 11 involves agreeing on final needs and selecting solution strategies. As such, it serves as the beginning of action planning, designated in Step 12. Similarly, immediately acting on doable solutions in the emerging plan ("picking the low-hanging fruit") means that implementing Step 13 often begins in Step 12 while the plan is still being developed. In Step 13, when full implementation is underway, successful action further enhances support for and commitment to the plan, thereby reinforcing Step 12. Finally, Step 13, monitoring progress of the implementation, flows into Step 14, documenting and evaluating the entire assessment. Keeping track of progress during the implementation helps determine where success is occurring and where adjustments are needed.

Much of what occurs in postassessment is process oriented, and skilled needs assessors must equip themselves with the tools necessary for the job. The following chapters contain information, strategies, and examples to assist needs assessors in doing just that—successfully facilitating postassessment in ways that get the results used for effective organizational change.

Highlights of the Chapter

An effective needs assessment requires much more than surveying perceptions, brainstorming actions, and mandating change. This chapter outlines key considerations for systematically and successfully conducting a full assessment.

1. Needs assessors should embrace the three-phase model.

2. They should keep three levels of needs (clients, service providers, and organizational systems) in mind throughout the assessment.

3. They should especially focus on particular levels of needs as the assessment progresses through its three phases (preassessment, needs assessment, and postassessment).

4. Postassessment (Phase III) focuses on three broad purposes: (a) prioritizing solution strategies derived from identified needs, (b) creating and implementing an action plan, and (c) documenting the implementation and evaluating the entire assessment.

5. Four steps provide a pathway to success: (a) making final decisions on needs and solution strategies, (b) creating/communicating an action plan and building commitment/support, (c) implementing and monitoring the plan, and (d) documenting and evaluating the entire assessment.

6. Effective postassessment requires knowledge of change and competencies for enacting it (interpersonal, technical, and facilitation skills).

7. The major challenges of postassessment include the complexity of change and the myriad of unexpected events that can influence the process.

2

The Nuts and Bolts of Postassessment

Gearing Up for the Journey

Thinking well is wise; planning well, wiser; but doing well is the wisest and best of all.

—Persian proverb

❖ INTRODUCTION

Conducting a comprehensive needs assessment is like blazing a trail through uncharted territory. Preassessment activities in the first phase of the journey provide initial grounding, enabling those on the needs assessment committee (NAC) to better see the lay of the land and make decisions about pursuing a formal expedition to obtain information on the existing state of affairs. Needs assessment is the second phase, through which additional information provides greater clarity about needs, possible solution strategies, and priorities for taking action. Postassessment, the last phase, enables those involved to make final decisions on solution strategies and then create, communicate, implement, and monitor an action plan in ways that build commitment and support for effective change.

It is tempting to think that once Phase II of the needs assessment process is complete, it is time to move to Phase III and focus on a plan of action. Not so fast! Preparation for postassessment plays an important role in accomplishing its ultimate goal of effective change within the organization. Such preplanning includes, again using the travel metaphor, putting together a team with the diverse skills needed for the journey, plotting a course, employing useful tools for navigation, developing systems of communication, and deciding how to document steps taken.

This chapter focuses on transitioning from needs assessment to postassessment in the three-phase model. First, we consider a number of lessons in organizational change useful for making the transition. We then consider important areas for decision making that will affect postassessment, including involvement, logistics, communication, and information management. Considering at the onset how to deal with these various concerns helps set the stage for a successful journey.

❖ ORGANIZATIONAL CHANGE

Fundamentally, postassessment is about developing, implementing, and monitoring an action plan for agreed-upon solution strategies that the organization will carry out. Simply stated, postassessment is aimed at positively affecting the future. The activities of needs assessment clarify the gap between desired and existing states; the activities of postassessment carry out solution strategies to close that gap. Focusing on factors that promote change, therefore, must play a central role in making preparations. Considerations include whom to involve, logistics, norms for communication, and information management. Wise needs assessors and organizational leaders will prepare for these in light of effective change.

The literature across numerous disciplines provides a wealth of information on factors and conditions associated with successful (or failed) initiatives for change, reform, restructuring, organization development, and so on (e.g., see Bolman & Deal, 2001, 2008; Fullan, 2006, 2007, 2008; Kotter & Cohen, 2002; Kouzes & Posner, 2007;

Pascale, Millemann, & Gioja, 2000; Pfeffer, 2007; Pfeffer & Sutton, 2000; Senge, 2006; Stacey, 1992, 1996, 2007; Wheatley, 2005). Although a comprehensive review is beyond our purpose here, the major challenge of change in a word is complexity. Numerous factors enter into any change effort, and countless forces—many of which are unforeseen—affect the process. For example, new laws or government regulations appear, budgets shift, a key leader leaves the organization, employees transfer to different departments, people retire, new hires come aboard, migration relocates populations, new technological inventions emerge, severe weather or natural disasters reorder priorities, and so on. Despite well-crafted plans and best intentions, there are no guarantees. So, what does this mean for those leading the postassessment process?

Experts advise us to start by appreciating and capitalizing on the complexity of change. Fullan (1993, 1999, 2003, 2008), for example, has presented several sets of change lessons over the years, each evolving as new empirical findings emerge. Although titles and terminology differ somewhat across these sets—from basic lessons to complex lessons to secrets of change and from mandates that can't motivate what matters to moral purpose that can to mobilization of moral purpose, quality relationships, and quality knowledge—the underlying imperative is to engage complexity, not lament it, try to tame it, or totally give up on it (all of which are futile). Instead, Fullan suggests investing in the power of people learning from and with each other as they apply substance (ideas, knowledge, data, materials, strategies, resources, technology) to a larger valued purpose (mission, vision, or what Fullan calls moral purpose). Leaders should involve and support all individuals in making new practices their own through problem solving issues unique to their contexts. This type of activity—collaboratively wrestling with the seeming chaos of complexity to better understand its meaning—leads to greater clarity, commitment, capacity, and coherence (all of which support effective practice and successful change).

Even after many years, Fullan's (1993) original eight basic lessons of change continue to guide postassessment usefully because they so well capture the complexity and tensions involved in the process (see Table 2.1). Each lesson is somewhat of a paradox, illuminating the fluctuating, unpredictable nature of change yet also providing direction for capitalizing on that dynamic to navigate pathways successfully.

Table 2.1 Eight Basic Lessons of Change

1. You can't mandate what matters.
2. Change is a journey, not a blueprint.
3. Problems are our friends.
4. Vision and strategic planning come later.
5. Individualism and collectivism must have equal power.
6. Neither centralization nor decentralization works.
7. Connection with the wider environment is critical for success.
8. Every person is a change agent.

Source: From Fullan, M. (1993). *Change forces: Probing the depths of educational reform,* pp. 21–22. London, UK: RoutledgeFalmer.

Let's consider the last lesson first: *Every person is a change agent.* Believing that everyone matters in the change process—embracing the reality that organizational change will happen only when committed individuals collectively take action—creates a different mindset for those leading postassessment efforts. Instead of creating and then trying to sell an action plan to organizational members, needs assessors and organizational leaders would do well to involve everyone within the organization in conversations about the plan— at best obtaining widespread input at the onset for its development and at least seeking reflective feedback about what it means once it has been developed. Such conversations focus on discovering the types of actions already underway that support the plan, personal concerns about implementing it, what resources individuals believe they need, and so on. Gaining commitment to a common plan requires meaningful engagement that enables people to personally construct their own understanding of the plan and their role in carrying it out.

Recognizing the vital role of individual participation in change also challenges us to think differently about mandates, blueprints, unexpected problems, and strategic planning. Fullan's (1993) first four lessons address these components: *You can't mandate what matters. Change is a journey, not a blueprint. Problems are our friends. Vision and strategic planning come later.* Combined, these lessons again emphasize the importance of all stakeholders throughout the entire process. Although mandates formalize policy—and should be established to clarify what an organization stands for—no mandate can force individuals to act in desirable ways. Instead, people must want and commit to carry out policies and procedures. Meaningful involvement, not detailed blueprints developed by others, builds commitment. At best a blueprint can map a route but only in general terms because actual pathways will be filled with unforeseen surprises—some helpful, others not—requiring adjustments for success. Realistically, people must develop details for any blueprint during the trip, largely by addressing problems that inevitably occur along the way. In fact, research in education reveals that getting stuck in strategic planning actually detracts from student achievement (Reeves, 2006, 2009). It is far better to devote less energy to mapping the perfect plan (which can never exist, no matter how thorough or visually pleasing the document) and more energy to carrying out actions in a concise one-page plan (which can be refined, elaborated, and further shaped as people learn through actual practice).

As the saying goes, problems become friends by revealing unexpected implementation challenges that must be addressed. Concerns that arise are integral to success because growth comes through reflecting on and learning from actions taken and determining necessary adjustments. This process contributes to developing greater clarity and sharper focus about the change effort itself. That is how vision and strategic planning collectively emerge. It's not that an initial action (or strategic) plan is worthless, but rather that such a plan is only a starting point. An experiential learning cycle unfolds as people plan, act, reflect, and revise. Conventional wisdom for effective planning dictates a "ready, aim, fire" approach, yet that sequence could derail change because people spend too much time planning rather than jumping in early and learning from the unavoidable challenges that arise. Alternatively, embracing a "ready, fire, aim" approach better positions those involved to learn early on what needs fine tuning and therefore move more effectively toward achieving successful change.

For example, one spring when a needs assessment documented that fourth- and fifth-grade teachers in a large district were overwhelmed with several new curriculum adoptions, the associate superintendent picked four schools to implement curriculum specialization the following fall. In those schools the fourth- and fifth-grade teachers reduced the number of core subjects they taught from four to two. There was little time for in-depth planning over the summer. Instead, the details of the needed professional development and coaching support evolved during the first year as teachers taught two sections rather than a self-contained classroom. Despite wrinkles in the implementation, by the end of the year most teachers supported the new assignment, believing that students were genuinely learning more, and specialization expanded to four additional schools the following year.

The fifth and sixth lessons focus attention on the importance of balance: *Individualism and collectivism must have equal power. Neither centralization nor decentralization works.* Individuals working in isolation can easily stray from a central organizational purpose by doing their own thing whereas collective efforts can easily miss the mark via groupthink. Effective leaders listen to and respect individual vision and innovation while enabling people to connect and direct their unique efforts to a larger collective purpose. Successful change is more likely when needs assessors embrace both top-down and bottom-up approaches, not one versus the other. Central authority, for example, can provide the focus, resources, and accountability necessary for supporting and sustaining change through stages of initiation, implementation, and institutionalization, while simultaneously encouraging and supporting decentralized innovation. Constant interaction between a defining center and satellite activities creates a healthy symbiotic balance.

Consider, for example, a clinic's program designed to train local teenagers to teach their peers about healthy living and potential risks to their health. The staff at the clinic wrote the training curriculum and materials, conducted the training, and sent the teens on their first round of interactions in the community. After a month, the staff and teens reviewed how the teaching had gone. Teens suggested revisions to both the process and the materials; the staff realized they needed to provide additional coaching support and a monitoring mechanism to track the individuals with whom the teens interacted. Working together collaboratively improved the implementation as "top-down" interacted with "bottom-up" ideas.

Finally, the seventh lesson reminds us that insular change efforts are likely to fail: *Connection with the wider environment is critical for success.* Internal development at the expense of external development will be counterproductive. Looking outward (staying plugged into the outside world) is just as important as looking inward (building capacity within the organization for ongoing development and productivity). Respecting both dimensions—akin to acting locally and thinking globally—better positions change efforts to address shifting conditions and take advantage of new ideas.

So, what does this all mean for transitioning from needs assessment to postassessment? Collectively, Fullan's (1993) eight lessons suggest that decisions about involvement, logistics, communication, and information management can—and should—be made with change in mind. For example, who should be involved in leading, coordinating, or managing postassessment processes? How can those leaders/coordinators/ managers maximize the participation of stakeholders at all levels in developing an action plan or at least in making meaning of the plan once it has been developed? How can the logistics of meetings, schedules, materials, and resources be leveraged for successful change? What norms for communication among stakeholders will best support change efforts? How can information management systems be established to assist in collecting, cataloging, storing, and retrieving documents? Addressing involvement, logistics, communication, and information management requires transition decisions that essentially establish solid foundations for accomplishing steps and tasks in postassessment. We discuss such decisions next.

❖ TRANSITION DECISIONS

Involvement

The major tasks of postassessment include (a) making final decisions about solution strategies, (b) developing and finalizing a plan, (c) disseminating and implementing the plan, (d) monitoring progress, and (e) evaluating effectiveness of the plan and the entire needs assessment. Deciding whom to engage in these tasks is important for successful change. To start, consider the size and structure of the organization, leaders/individuals in its units, the nature of solution strategies, and the structural framework in place during the assessment.

The lessons of change presented earlier suggest inclusive and strategic involvement. Inclusive involvement recognizes that, ultimately, individuals collectively make change. Meaningfully involving individuals in postassessment, therefore, makes change more likely. In small organizations, it may be possible to include everyone in all of the tasks of postassessment. Realistically, however, some form of representative participation will be necessary in most cases, especially in mid- to large-sized and multisite organizations. Strategically, leaders in the hierarchy (chief executive officers, superintendents, division managers, department heads, program directors, unit leaders, etc.) must be on board because they occupy positions of authority. Those who approve the allocation of resources must also be involved because they literally can bring any change effort to a grinding halt by enacting counterproductive policies, failing to champion solution strategies, or denying access to necessary resources.

We suggest revisiting the map that depicts organizational structure (or constructing one if it doesn't exist) to review the terrain. Look at individuals who occupy leadership positions on the chart and then identify others (regardless of position) who will be integral to the change effort. The latter are those well respected by colleagues who possess the expertise and skills necessary for supporting the tasks of postassessment and executing solution strategies. These individuals may be frontrunners for change or possibly opponents. Cross-sectional representation of all stakeholders and organizational units will be important to the eventual success of the change effort.

Next, consider the structural framework that was in place during Phase II of the needs assessment. Prepare a visual diagram that shows the various committees or groups that conducted the assessment. Typically the NAC guided the process and may have been responsible for collecting and analyzing data, or a separate data collection team (DCT) may have been established to perform that role. Review the established framework to determine (a) if those same committees should be maintained during Phase III, (b) if additional committees or teams might be useful, (c) who should serve on committees, and (d) how committees should interface with each other and with the organization. Depending on whether the proposed changes are relatively small/minor versus large/intricate or require short- versus long-term effort, it may be useful to establish a separate action planning team (APT) and/or progress assessment team (PAT), both of which would regularly report to the NAC. On the other hand, the NAC (after fine-tuning membership) may be the group that actually develops an action plan based on the needs and solution strategies previously identified. We suggest first determining who will serve on the NAC during postassessment and then considering whether other committees will be helpful. A worksheet for planning NAC membership appears in Figure 2.1.

Although we caution against too many committees that could add unnecessary bureaucratic layers, we do suggest considering if additional groups would promote the involvement necessary for

Figure 2.1 NAC Membership

Directions:

A. Keep the NAC <u>size</u> manageable (5–10 people).

B. Plan appropriate <u>representation</u>.
- Review the structure of the needs assessment context (organizational chart).
- Consider sites/locations (single or multiple).
- Consider departments/units (subdivisions).

C. Consider a range of <u>roles</u>.

D. Involve people over a continuum of <u>tenure</u> (established and new members).

E. Pay attention to the <u>expertise</u> that individuals will bring to the NA process.

Name	Representation		Role				Tenure		Expertise					
	Site/Location	Department/Unit	Leader/Director	Staff/Service Provider	Client/Service Recipient	Other Stakeholders	Established	New	Evaluation	Change Facilitation	Interpersonal	Communication	Intercultural	Technology
1.														
2.														
3.														
4.														
5.														
6.														
7.														
8.														
9.														
10.														

successful change and the extent to which those groups should overlap. The purpose of each committee should be clearly articulated and interconnections among functions clearly explicated so that participants can make meaning of their roles in the postassessment effort and maximize contributions toward carrying out the tasks necessary for success. Effective decision making here requires recognizing the value of widespread participation across stakeholders in postassessment while maintaining a streamlined structure for enacting the process—a delicate dance, indeed.

Logistics

Attending to logistics during postassessment also underpins progress toward successful organizational change. Logistics, such as keeping a calendar, scheduling committee meetings, preparing agendas, documenting tasks, providing needed resources, organizing materials, supplying technology, and arranging/maintaining both clerical and technical support, are the nuts and bolts of postassessment. Other logistical concerns may surface throughout postassessment, but think about these basics at the beginning. Establishing normative routines and agreed-upon ways to manage logistics typically proves to be helpful, if people realize that adjustments may be necessary to address unforeseen problems or new circumstances that occur along the way.

First, decide who will manage logistics, one person or several. Responsibilities may include maintaining the calendar and meeting schedules, providing agendas and "to do" lists, attending to technology needs, and so forth. If several people fulfill these roles, our suggestion is that someone be designated as the point person for a coordinated system. In deciding who specifically should take on coordination tasks, consider personal skills, styles, and strengths of potential candidates. Being able to organize systematically, follow up consistently, attend to details, keep accurate records, and work with others are the *sine qua non* for success; without these, success is unlikely.

In addition, keep in mind that logistics can facilitate or frustrate involvement, increase or decrease commitment, and enhance or complicate problem solving. Preplanning common sets of expectations and user-friendly procedures helps establish norms for consistency, especially in light of the fact that change often creates uncertainty and anxiety. We suggest that those who manage logistics adhere to the following guidelines:

1. Set regular meetings.

2. Choose a convenient, easily accessible location and use it consistently.

3. Develop and repeatedly use templates for meeting agendas, "to do" lists, and other tasks that committees will perform.

4. Preplan a system for organizing documents and other resource materials.

5. Establish procedures that can be carried out routinely to accomplish set expectations.

6. Reinforce established norms by recording, distributing, reviewing frequently, and revising as necessary agreed-upon procedures.

7. Provide all committee members with tabbed notebooks for templates/documents, along with access to shared electronic sites/folders/files that contain these materials.

Think about how best to schedule meetings. Setting a routine schedule good for all members of a committee (rather than scheduling irregularly or meeting by meeting) can enhance attendance by allowing participants to better manage their individual calendars. For example, a committee may consistently meet from 9:00 a.m. to 10:30 a.m. the first and third Tuesday of every month. In single-site situations (or with electronic conferencing capabilities across multiple sites) it may be advantageous to meet more frequently for shorter periods of time to foster greater ongoing communication. If possible, use a consistent location that is easily accessible and most convenient for all committee members. Also systematically send out meeting reminders the week before as well as the day before.

Next, anticipate the types of procedural forms and documents that will be used frequently throughout postassessment. For example, certain tasks will be ongoing or repeated. Create templates for these to streamline recordkeeping and communication. Such documents include meeting agendas and minutes (see Figure 2.2), "to do" lists (see Figure 2.3), and reflection or feedback forms (see Figure 2.4). Other templates include a generic outline for the action plan that will eventually be developed (see Figures 2.5 and 2.6) and a timetable for its implementation (see Figure 2.7). These are common tools that orient committees toward tasks, provide normative structures for accomplishment, and promote consistent ways of communicating.

Figure 2.2   Meeting Agenda

	Meeting Date: *Year-Month-Day*
Organization Name *Mission Statement*	

Committee Name

Date _____
Time _____
Place _____

Committee Members
("X" indicates those present)

❑ Name _____   ❑ Name _____   ❑ Name _____

❑ Name _____   ❑ Name _____   ❑ Name _____

❑ Name _____   ❑ Name _____   ❑ Name _____

Agenda Items	Action Minutes
1. Check In (welcome, warm up, connect, report/discuss reflections from last meeting)	Topic/Input
2. Review/Correct/Approve minutes from last meeting	Corrections/Approved
3. Review/Finalize current agenda	Input/Revisions
4. Review/Update "To Do" list	A. Issue/Item: B. Input/Discussion: C. Decision/Rationale:
5. Review/Update other standing issues/items (list and number each in the same order at each meeting)	A. Issue/Item: B. Input/Discussion: C. Decision/Rationale:
6. Parking lot items (for later discussion)	A. Issue/Item: B. Input/Discussion: C. Decision/Rationale:
7. Closure (reflections, pluses/wishes, lessons learned)	Collect/Summarize

Source: © 2000 Laurie Stevahn & Jean A. King.

Figure 2.3 "To Do" List

			Meeting Date: *Year-Month-Day*
	Committee Name **"To Do" List** **Date** _____		
Task **(description)**	**Who** **(person** **responsible)**	**Target Date** **(for** **completion)**	**Current Status** **(progress/completed)**
1.			
2.			
3.			
4.			
5.			
6.			
7.			
8.			
9.			

Source: © 2000 Laurie Stevahn & Jean A. King.

Figure 2.4 Meeting Reflections

Meeting Reflections **Date** _____		
Pluses **What did you like,** **appreciate, value?**	*Wishes* **What do you wish** **had been different?**	*Questions* **What questions** **remain? Ask them!**
Thanks for your input!		

Source: © 2000 Laurie Stevahn & Jean A. King.

Figure 2.5   Action Plan

Draft/Final Date: *Year-Month-Day*
Organization Name Mission Statement **Needs Assessment Action Plan** Date _____
Purpose and Rationale (overall aim and reasons for the action plan)
Summary of the Planning Process (overview of steps in the process)
Action Plan Committee Members (names of participants)
Issue I *Goal 1* Actions A, B, C, etc. *Goal 2* Actions A, B, C, etc. *Goal 3* Actions A, B, C, etc.
Issue II *Goal 1* Actions A, B, C, etc. *Goal 2* Actions A, B, C, etc. *Goal 3* Actions A, B, C, etc.
Issue III *Goal 1* Actions A, B, C, etc. *Goal 2* Actions A, B, C, etc. *Goal 3* Actions A, B, C, etc.

Source: © 2006 Laurie Stevahn.

Figure 2.6 One-Page Action Plan

	Draft/Final Date: *Year-Month-Day*

Organization Name
Mission Statement
Needs Assessment Action Plan
Date _____

Purpose and Rationale	**Summary of the Planning Process**	**Action Plan Committee Members**
(reasons why the needs assessment was conducted)	(major action planning steps)	(names of participants)
• • • • •	1. 2. 3. 4. 5.	_____ _____ _____ _____ _____ _____ _____ _____ _____ _____

Issue/Need	Solution Strategy	Goals	Actions
Issue I	1.	A. _____ B. _____	a. b. c. _____ a. b. c. _____
	2.	A. _____ B.	a. b. _____ a. b.
Issue II	1.	A. _____ B.	a. b. _____ a. b.
Issue III	1.	A.	a. b. c. d. e.

Source: © 2006 Laurie Stevahn.

Figure 2.7   Action Plan Timetable

Action Plan Timetable

Date _____

Issue Number	Goal Number	Action Number	Task	Time Targets			Responsible Parties (Coordinators)
				Begin	Continue	Complete	

Source: © 2006 Laurie Stevahn.

Finally, preplan a system for organizing, storing, and accessing the documents generated and resources used in postassessment. Common expectations and jointly understood procedures help avoid the chaos that can emerge quickly when individuals in one or more committees are making their own unique contributions toward producing and implementing change. Consider who will be responsible for maintaining files and/or archives (electronic and paper copies), what classification schemes will be easiest for labeling and storing documents, and who will have access to materials. A helpful system will standardize procedures to prevent ambiguity and pave the way for smooth operations. It also will affect communication networks and information management, both of which can make or break effective change.

Communication

Many believe, with good reason, that the overall effectiveness or health of an organization has as much to do with its communication norms and networks as with anything else. In short, the culture of communication that characterizes an organization ("how we do business around here") defines the organization in substantive ways—something akin to "you are what you eat." In a perfect world, open, honest, responsive, respectful, culturally competent, and continuous communication would allow everyone including leaders and managers, service providers and support staff, and clients and other stakeholders alike to engage productively in postassessment. However, communication issues and/or difficulties are frequently at the heart of organizational woes, program difficulties, or identified needs. This creates a tremendous challenge for postassessment—the needs assessment phase that especially requires effective communication and collaboration to achieve change. Less-than-effective communication (which may already exist) will frustrate efforts and threaten, if not totally sabotage, success. Consider the following examples:

- Several individuals, each representing different yet related programs within a department, fail to communicate to colleagues new departmental policies that were adopted to better facilitate various provisions in the postassessment action plan.
- Program personnel make a structural change to better serve clients as specified by the action plan yet fail to inform administrative assistants who often are the first people contacted by program recipients or prospective clients seeking information.

- A program director sends a newsletter to service recipients about upcoming changes prior to alerting or seeking input from service providers who must carry out the changes.
- An angry client files a complaint with a governing board about a licensed practitioner who changes protocol, unaware that new procedures were put in place to implement the action plan.

Each of these situations reveals problems with communication during postassessment, perhaps symptomatic of those that existed within the organization prior to the assessment of needs. Clear and timely communication may help prevent such complications, along with the frustration and ill will that often result. Although changing communication patterns doesn't happen overnight, needs assessors can take steps to head off disasters.

Establishing agreed-upon communication protocols and vigilantly adhering to them in postassessment can begin to transform problematic patterns. To do this, needs assessors should target five areas for communication protocols.

1. *Communication within committees.* All postassessment committees (NAC, DCT, APT, etc.) should establish, use, and monitor the effectiveness of a set of working norms for communication among members. We suggest those listed in Figure 2.8. Invite committee members to add others deemed important for maintaining effective communication and positive interpersonal relations. Post the list at each meeting and periodically reflect on which norms are working well and which need adjusting. Also consider designating someone on the committee to be responsible for regular follow-up.

Figure 2.8 Working Norms

- Seek all voices; involve everyone.
- Listen respectfully; communicate understanding.
- Explore alternatives; don't jump to conclusions.
- Raise issues constructively; engage in positive problem solving.
- Appreciate each person's unique histories, perspectives, talents, and skills.
- Assume confidentiality; what's discussed in the meeting stays in the meeting.
- Mutually agree on information to be shared with others outside of the meeting.

Source: © 2000 Laurie Stevahn.

2. *Communication among committees.* If multiple committees have been established, it will be helpful to determine general guidelines for communication among them. How will information be shared? Perhaps committee chairs (or a designated committee member) will be the ones to provide updates systematically to the other committees via an agreed-upon method such as electronic postings or hard-copy summaries. It may be prudent to determine if all committee members simultaneously receive information/decisions or if committee chairs first receive communications and then forward those messages to committee members. The fewer postassessment committees, the greater the potential for more manageable communication. This may be an important factor in determining how many committees to establish. Remember the KISS principle (Keep It Short and Simple). Adding layers to already existing bureaucracy may be counterproductive and heighten frustration, thereby easily detracting from efforts to foster and sustain positive interpersonal relationships required for postassessment processes.

3. *Communication beyond committees.* Sometimes committees should share information with others not directly charged with postassessment activities (administrative hierarchies within the organization, departments or units, service providers across programs or divisions, clients or program/service recipients, governing or advisory boards, evaluation or program funders, other branches of the organization in multisite situations, the community/society at large, or other stakeholders). Those spearheading postassessment efforts should develop policies, guidelines, and procedures for such communications. Will the chair of the NAC (or some other designated participant) be responsible for communicating information? Will there be opportunities for NAC members to consider and/or provide feedback on written communications before release to wider audiences? What avenues for responding should those who receive information use?

4. *Electronic communication.* Electronics can provide numerous advantages when it comes to communication. Needs assessors and/or postassessment committees can share information among themselves (and with organizational staff and other stakeholders) rapidly, efficiently, and inexpensively. They can also obtain input easily and quickly—whether from a few or many via e-mail or electronic user-friendly surveys. Online

chats, threaded discussions, video streams, and other interactive technology make connections more accessible than ever. These advantages also come with potential pitfalls, such as when everyone does not have appropriate hardware, software, or online access; e-mail overload becomes all-consuming; new software or application updates make it difficult to access old files or merge new ones; individuals name files or folders differently, which complicates storage and retrieval; and so on. Again, it is wise to set guidelines for electronic communication just as for other forms of communication.

Electronic protocol might include (a) naming folders/files (by date, title, committee name, person responsible, or other agreed-upon options), (b) posting items on shared directories (meeting minutes, "to do" lists, draft documents, or other information), (c) responding to e-mail messages (reply to sender only, reply to all, reply using an electronic mailing list), and (d) using e-mail versus face-to-face communication (such as for short concrete messages, agenda distribution prior to meetings, and simple feedback rather than complex substantive communications). Discussing complex, emotionally charged, or political issues in face-to-face meetings, rather than electronically, tends to facilitate change by fostering the kinds of dialogue and conversation necessary for the in-depth exploration of ideas, immediate clarification for understanding, sensitivity to personal perspectives, attention to cultural nuances, and use of nonverbal cues (facial expressions, body postures, hand gestures)—all of which affect how individuals make meaning.

5. *Confidentiality.* Think carefully about confidentiality. Trust is a necessary component for change; people won't take risks without it. Transparency can foster trust, but it also can work against confidentiality. Appreciate the tension between confidentiality and transparency. Agree upon what information, documents, and files must be kept confidential and what can be freely shared. Doing so will not guarantee smooth sailing but may help avert or diminish the negative effects that conflicts over confidentiality could bring. This becomes especially important for those who have access to raw data (members of the DCT, those responsible for data entry, anyone involved in data analysis). Be clear and firm regarding data confidentiality.

Communication is a big concern in nearly all human endeavors, and needs assessment is no exception. Although dealing with all aspects of communication goes beyond the scope of this text, gearing up to plan and implement solution strategies that address identified needs in postassessment requires paying attention to the communication issues noted above. While we do not suggest trying to micromanage every aspect of communication in postassessment—which would be absurd, impossible, and unhelpful—we do advocate developing systematic routines and guidelines for communication at the start of postassessment to enhance the entire process.

Information Management

Managing information overlaps somewhat with communication. Here the focus is on documentation and recordkeeping. Postassessment processes produce documentation valuable for future initiatives. Transitioning from Phase II to Phase III presents an opportune time to ensure that an audit trail is in place, easy for others to follow. Every needs assessment develops its own history; recording it serves numerous purposes. Documentation is useful for reflecting on actions and refining processes, reinforcing a culture of data-based decision making, promoting evaluation capacity building, bringing newcomers on board or stakeholders not directly involved in committee work up to speed, providing concrete evidence of what transpired if questions about procedure or accuracy arise, and so on. We provide three tips for information management when transitioning into postassessment.

First, don't launch into postassessment (Phase III) without putting needs assessment (Phase II) documentation in order. This may include collecting and organizing items such as (a) a chronological timetable of the various steps that were taken to determine needs; (b) records of committees, participants, meeting minutes, issues/decisions/rationales, and so on; (c) sampling procedures; (d) data collection methods and instruments; (e) raw data files; (f) data analysis strategies; (g) identified needs; (h) solutions considered; and (i) priority decisions, along with other pertinent forms or materials. The goal is to tell the story of the needs assessment so that a detailed record exists and reflection may occur to enhance future practice. In this way, it becomes an organizational learning tool that goes beyond solely being useful for determining needs; documenting the process also promotes evaluation capacity building, enabling those involved to further develop the skills of gathering and using data to address questions of importance to the organization.

Second, take time to facilitate conversations about lessons learned in NAC meetings and other stakeholder groups. Revisit and review collected documents to reflect on procedures and forms, database management, use of resources, project decisions, and so on. Discuss questions such as "What worked well?" "What did not?" and "What refinements would be helpful for future projects?" These conversations throughout needs assessment generate an invaluable record of "Do's" and "Don't's"—some of which can immediately be put into play when gearing up for postassessment. Remember that dealing with problems is part of growth; you can't learn without them. Documenting difficulties helps ensure that what we learn from problems is not lost but instead integrated into ongoing practice. This also becomes an important part of evaluating the entire needs assessment at its end, the last step in the postassessment process (see Chapter 6).

Third, decide how to label folders and files for storing/archiving documents. Create a table of contents (or tracking sheet) that lists such information. Maintain electronic and paper copies of documents and determine where they will be housed (specific offices, central vs. secluded locations, protected vs. open environments, locked cabinets or password-only files vs. shared storage options). Determine who has access to stored documents. Discuss confidentiality issues along with ethical, legal, political, or situational circumstances that might influence choices and then make thoughtful decisions. Appoint someone with expert organizational skills to summarize protocols, collect documents, and manage files.

Highlights of the Chapter

Transitioning from Phase II to Phase III in needs assessment entails taking stock of all that has transpired and making decisions in light of what we know about change to promote success during postassessment. This chapter outlines factors that, for better or worse, will influence the course of postassessment. Wise needs assessors will attend to each.

1. Recognize that postassessment fundamentally deals with change, which entails developing an action plan to implement solution strategies for identified needs.

2. Appreciate the complexity of change. Despite no guarantees for success, applying what we know about enabling and impeding factors can help keep the process on track.

3. Consider Fullan's (1993) eight basic lessons of change: (a) Mandates don't work, (b) the journey takes time, (c) learn from problems that surface

along the way, (d) shift from "plans" to "actions" earlier rather than later, (e) connect individual uniqueness with collective purpose, (f) balance centralized and decentralized support, (g) plug into the wider environment, and (h) view all as agents for change.

4. Determine protocols for involvement, logistics, communication, and information management. Involvement concerns postassessment committees and their membership, recognizing the value of both widespread participation/representation and streamlined structures/operations. Logistics concern meeting schedules, locations, resources, document templates, and other nuts-and-bolts routines. Communication concerns interaction mechanisms within, among, and beyond committees, along with electronic options and confidentiality issues. Information management concerns creating a comprehensive, systematic, well-organized, user-friendly, transparent paper trail while simultaneously respecting appropriate confidentiality.

5. Create a foundation for ongoing organizational learning by documenting all aspects of the needs assessment before jumping into the postassessment phase.

3

The Action Plan

Collaborating for Change

Recognize that all successful [change] strategies are socially based and action oriented.

—Fullan, 2006, p. 44

❖ INTRODUCTION

Successful expeditions require teamwork. Whether climbing Mount Everest, navigating the Amazon, or cycling in the Tour de France, teamwork wins the day. The same is true for postassessment. Developing and implementing an action plan requires the constructive participation and sustained commitment of those who work in the organization. In fact, needs assessors and organizational leaders must meaningfully invite, involve, ignite, and interconnect people in ways that will get the results used. This is the heart of postassessment—using needs assessment information to bring about meaningful change.

The good news is that research on organization development and effective change provides valuable knowledge for leading and managing the process. Simply stated, collaboration among organizational members working toward a shared purpose or mission is the foundation for success. The bad news is that change is a complex process fraught with unexpected twists and turns as the journey unfolds. Like a roller coaster, preplanned tracks provide direction, but highs, lows, and varying speeds along the way can produce a somewhat chaotic experience. Roller coasters, however, eventually transport riders to a desired destination. Change efforts in postassessment hold no such guarantee.

We begin by discussing dimensions of successful organizational change. Those dimensions provide a rationale for using group strategies to carry out the steps of postassessment. We then offer 24 procedures to accomplish four broad purposes integral to creating and implementing the needs assessment action plan. Those purposes include (a) promoting positive interpersonal relations, (b) developing shared understandings, (c) prioritizing and finalizing decisions, and (d) assessing progress. Finally, we include step-by-step directions for facilitating the double dozen strategies and illustrate how they may be used to collaboratively create, implement, and assess an action plan.

❖ USING NEEDS ASSESSMENT FINDINGS TO MAKE CHANGE

The main objective of postassessment is to enable those within the organization to constructively use needs assessment information. The action plan grounds and guides this effort. A useful plan will specify solution strategies selected to address prioritized needs. It will also address implementation by outlining processes for enacting, monitoring, and evaluating the plan. For example, the plan should list tasks to accomplish each solution strategy, persons responsible, timelines, and mechanisms for assessing progress. Success, however, will depend not only on the substance of the plan but also on the facilitation procedures used to create and carry it out. People who understand foundations of change lead the way by strategically employing facilitation procedures intentionally designed to support change efforts.

Foundations of Change

On the surface, change is quite simple. Change occurs when individuals act in new ways, use resources differently, and express new understandings about their practice (Fullan, 2007). These external dimensions are easily observable and, in part, can be measures of progress. Yet change is anything but easy or simple. In fact, its complexity can be daunting. Internal dimensions often include feelings of discomfort, uncertainty, confusion, sense of loss, and sometimes ineffectiveness that individuals experience in the midst of doing things differently. Change requires people to let go of comfortable routines and embrace new norms for "how we do business around here." This can produce mild anxiety, at a minimum, or be quite threatening at the extreme.

Fundamentally, change is the story of how people individually and collectively work through concerns, fears, or anxieties as they engage in new practices, develop fluency with new skills, and embrace new understandings about what constitutes effectiveness (Fullan, 2007). In fact, struggling with concerns and questions is the process through which people grow by making meaning of the new practices they are being asked to carry out. Grappling with the following questions becomes instrumental in this transformative process:

- What exactly is the goal?
- Why is it important?
- What does it mean to me?
- What will it require of me?
- What skills and unique talents am I already using to advance it?
- What additional skills or training do I need?
- How will others support my efforts?
- How am I linked to others in accomplishing the goal?
- How will we know that we are making progress?
- What concerns do I have relevant to achieving this goal?
- What's in it for me?
- How will the organization benefit?
- How will our clients benefit?

Needs assessors and organizational leaders play significant roles in creating opportunities for implementers to grapple with these questions, thereby making sense of new policies and practices. Leaders, for example, can encourage people to jump in and try new implementations without reprisal, provide user-friendly mechanisms for individual reflection on the results, and institute ongoing collective dialogue on what the change means for personal practice and organizational effectiveness. Over time this transformative process results in qualitatively different ways of thinking, acting, and caring.

Five factors increase the likelihood of success. First, *collaboration* matters. Systematically and interactively engaging individuals in making meaning and developing skills becomes the bedrock for individual and organizational transformation. Second, *facilitation* matters. Those who coordinate postassessment steering committees or engage staff and clients in change activities nurture progress by using procedures that foster constructive social interaction. Third, *mission* matters. Individual and collaborative postassessment efforts should advance a clearly articulated larger purpose, the organization's reason for being. Mutual commitment to change has a better chance of growing when people see how the new actions they are being asked to implement contribute to the core goals and values of the organization. Fourth, *knowledge of change* matters. Equipping everyone with knowledge of the change process creates shared expectations for the journey, thereby enabling everyone to better manage and participate in change initiatives. Fifth, *leadership* matters. Leaders in key administrative positions within the organization who champion change—embrace, model, facilitate, reward, and celebrate it—signal and demonstrate direction by simultaneously walking the talk and talking the walk. Such leaders place their integrity on the line, standing firm for change while opening pathways for others to do likewise. Despite unexpected forces that can derail any postassessment effort (see Chapters 4 and 5), strong leaders who keep organizational mission at the forefront, facilitate collaboration in creating and implementing the action plan, and equip everyone with knowledge of change create conditions for success.

Facilitation for Change

Those who understand foundations of change bring a new mind-set to facilitating the steps of postassessment outlined in Table 1.3. That mind-set includes intentionally seeking and using facilitation procedures that meaningfully engage stakeholders throughout the process. A host of participant-centered, interactive, collaborative, and cooperative procedures exist, some validated by a wealth of empirical research, others deemed best practice by long histories of effective use (e.g., see Bennett & Rolheiser, 2001; D. W. Johnson & F. P. Johnson, 2009; Joyce, Weil, & Calhoun, 2009). Those presented in Table 3.1 especially enable needs assessors and organizational leaders to successfully involve stakeholders in finalizing priority needs, selecting solution strategies, creating the action plan, and then implementing, monitoring, and evaluating it.

The real value of these facilitation procedures is that they simultaneously accomplish multiple outcomes, all contributing to successful postassessment. One set of outcomes entails achieving the steps of postassessment noted above. A second set attends to the foundations of change. These procedures result in activities that involve stakeholders in figuring out what change means as they individually and collectively

Table 3.1 Postassessment Procedures and Purposes

Procedures / Purposes	A. Promoting Positive Interpersonal Relations	B. Developing Shared Understandings	C. Prioritizing and Finalizing Decisions	D. Assessing Progress
1. Voicing Variables	X			X
2. Voicing Viewpoints	X			X
3. Choosing Corners	X			X
4. Making Metaphors	X			X
5. Cooperative Interviews	X			X
6. Roundtable/Roundrobin	X			X
7. Check-In/Tune-In	X			X
8. Pluses/Wishes	X			X
9. PMI (Pluses/Minuses/Inquiries)/ PPP (Positives/Problems/ Possibilities)	X			X
10. Jigsaw		X		X
11. Graffiti/Carousel		X		X
12. Concept Formation		X		X
13. Concept Mapping/Mind Mapping		X		X
14. Force Field Analysis		X		X
15. Fishbone Analysis		X		X
16. What? So What? Now What?		X		X
17. Rubric Reflections		X		X

(Continued)

Table 3.1 (Continued)

Procedures / Purposes	A. Promoting Positive Interpersonal Relations	B. Developing Shared Understandings	C. Prioritizing and Finalizing Decisions	D. Assessing Progress
18. Fist to Five			X	X
19. Dot Voting			X	X
20. Bar Graphs			X	X
21. Cooperative Rank Order			X	X
22. Multi-Attribute Consensus Reaching (MACR)			X	X
23. Delphi Method/Nominal Group Technique			X	X
24. Constructive Controversy			X	X

Source: © 2001 Laurie Stevahn & Jean A. King.

grapple with implementation concerns, try out new behaviors, forge new understandings, and, through the process, come to value and commit to new norms of practice.

A third set of outcomes involves four broad facilitation purposes shown in Table 3.1. The procedures in Column A promote positive interpersonal relations among people doing the work of postassessment. Those in Column B result in shared understandings that ground subsequent decisions. Those in Column C deal directly with decision making by engaging participants in prioritizing and finalizing plans. Finally, Column D indicates that all of the procedures may be used to assess how well the needs assessment action plan is being implemented. Some are especially useful for collecting data on effectiveness, others for interpreting results. Some require little time and few resources, others more time and preparation (see Table 3.2). Together,

Table 3.2 Facilitation Time

																								Procedure
Time	1	2	3	4	5	6	7	8	9	10	11	12	13	14	15	16	17	18	19	20	21	22	23	24
Shorter 5–20 minutes	X	X	X	X	X	X	X	X	X		X							X	X	X				
Moderate 30–60 minutes											X	X	X	X	X	X	X				X			
Longer 1–2 hours										X											X	X	X	X

Source: © 2001 Laurie Stevahn & Jean A. King.

these procedures and their outcomes provide concrete ways to accomplish the steps of postassessment outlined in Table 1.3, as well as bring to life factors that influence effective change, especially making meaning of new expectations and collaborating for coordinated action.

Sometimes the needs assessment committee (NAC) coordinator will facilitate various procedures to engage members in finalizing solution strategies and creating the overall action plan. At other times organizational leaders, administrators, or managers will use the procedures to disseminate and garner support for the plan, develop commitment from staff, or assess effectiveness. Needs assessors also will employ these procedures, knowing that personal and meaningful involvement of leaders, staff, and clients promotes effective change. Regardless of who facilitates these activities, successful postassessment to a large degree will depend on constructively involving those charged with making change throughout the journey. These procedures become tools for making that happen. In the next section, we provide directions for facilitating the double dozen procedures and further elaborate on their targeted purposes. These descriptions focus on inexpensive face-to-face interaction that any facilitator can use; where technology is available (e.g., electronic response systems), facilitators may choose to adapt the procedures.

❖ PROCEDURES AND PURPOSES

Promoting Positive Interpersonal Relations

Positive interpersonal relations among those involved in postassessment activities contribute to productive collaborations in which individuals join together to achieve the work of change. An interpersonal climate of safety, trust, respect, belonging, and appreciation underpins success. It also provides a foundation for constructively managing controversies or conflicts that inevitably will occur as the change effort unfolds (see Chapter 4).

Positive relationships develop over time, as do effective groups. In fact, classic stage theories (e.g., Tuckman, 1965; Tuckman & Jensen, 1977) illustrate the evolving nature of groups as they *form, storm, norm, perform,* and *adjourn.* Making comfortable, respectful, meaningful interpersonal connections at the onset helps create a social environment that nurtures healthy development. Such connections promote mutual sharing, listening, exploring, clarifying, and valuing, even when people hold diverse beliefs or perspectives. Psychologists generally describe this process as a dynamic between self-disclosure and attentive responding, from which trusting and caring relationships evolve:

> By letting you know me, I allow you to like me. By disclosing myself to you, I create the potential for trust, caring, commitment, growth, self-understanding, and friendship. How can you care for me if you do not know me? How can you trust me if I do not demonstrate my trust in you by disclosing myself to you? How can you be committed to me if you know little or nothing about me? How can I know and understand myself if I do not disclose myself to friends? To like me, to trust me, to be committed to our relationship, to facilitate my personal growth and self-understanding, and to be my friend you must know me. (Johnson, 1997, p. 31)

Procedures 1–9 in Table 3.1 promote positive interpersonal relations by providing structured opportunities to reveal thoughts, ideas, values, beliefs, and life stories to others who likely will respond in ways that respect the vulnerability inherent in such sharing. Directions for facilitating these procedures appear in Figures 3.1–3.9. Some promote unity by enabling people to discover commonalities such as mutual identities (allegiance to a sports team), shared values (passion for a social cause), or similar experiences (travel adventures abroad). Others foster admiration by enabling people to learn about unique qualities, characteristics, or circumstances. For example, people marvel when they realize that someone in their midst possesses an unusual talent (champion yodeler), survived a dangerous situation (house fire), or participated in an extraordinary event (historic inauguration).

Positive relationships are too important in postassessment to be left to chance. That is why facilitators should become skilled in using procedures that enable people to make comfortable connections whenever groups gather to work on tasks. Whether a committee is meeting for the first time or has met many times, intentionally structuring meaningful interactions helps pave the way for collaboration. We recommend selecting and applying Procedures 1–9 when groups newly form and also thereafter at the start of every regularly scheduled meeting. For example, consider a needs assessor in an urban development program. The first meeting of the reconstituted NAC is about to begin. After welcoming and introducing everyone, the assessor reviews the steps of postassessment, orients the committee toward its targeted goal, and then facilitates *Procedure 1: Voicing Variables* (see Figure 3.1). The activity begins by announcing a variable and a range of possible responses. Individuals

Figure 3.1   Procedure 1: Voicing Variables

Procedure	Voicing Variables
Purpose	Promote positive interpersonal relations; identify personal characteristics
Time	5 minutes
Materials	• List of variables and responses (see samples below)
Directions	1. Welcome participants to the committee; briefly review history/background of the needs assessment and the committee's role. 2. Specify ultimate goals of the committee (create, implement, assess the needs assessment action plan), review the meeting agenda (see Figure 2.2), and agree upon working norms (see Figure 2.8). 3. Pose this question: "Who are we?" 4. Specify a variable (such as place of birth) and then read aloud a list of possible responses (such as North America, South America, Europe, Africa, Middle East, Asia, Australia, Pacific Islands); ask participants to stand (or raise hands) for the option that personally applies. 5. Note similarities and differences among response options; estimate percentages for each option; highlight those that support productive committee work (such as similar core values, useful technical skills, or past work experiences, all of which promote success).
Applications	Sample Variables/Responses Birthplace/Hometown: (USA) Northeast, Midwest, Southeast, South/Texas, Pacific Northwest, Southwest/California, Alaska/Hawaii; (non-USA) name continents and then ask what country Job/Role/Position: Administrator, service provider, clerical/support staff, evaluator/researcher, HRD/trainer, public relations, client, other Joined the Organization/Program: Within the past 5 years, 10 years, 15 years, 20 years, 25 years, more than a

	quarter-century ago (or in the first decade of the 21st century, 1990s, 1980s, 1970s, 1960s, 1950s, earlier) Favorite Tasks/Skills: Designing projects, teaching/mentoring, working with technology, maintaining databases, collaborating, leading initiatives, evaluating progress, analyzing issues, synthesizing information Ideal Vacation Spot: Tropical beach, mountain resort, world-class city

Figure 3.2   Procedure 2: Voicing Viewpoints

Procedure	Voicing Viewpoints
Purpose	Promote positive interpersonal relations; reveal values and clarify assumptions
Time	5–10 minutes per viewpoint statement
Materials	• *Voicing Viewpoints* sheet (one per participant; each sheet contains several viewpoint statements on topics relevant to postassessment; see samples below)
Directions	1. Distribute the *Voicing Viewpoints* sheet. 2. Read each viewpoint statement; ask participants to circle the response option that personally applies. 3. Facilitate whole-session discussion on each statement systematically by asking participants to raise hands: "How many circled Strongly Agree? Agree? Disagree? Strongly Disagree?" Estimate response percentages for each option. 4. Ask participants to share reasons underlying their varied responses; compare and contrast. Focus on what the reasons reveal about people's backgrounds, experiences, and assumptions important for accomplishing postassessment tasks. 5. Discuss what the viewpoint statements and responses mean for successful postassessment.

(Continued)

Figure 3.2 (Continued)

Applications	Sample Viewpoint Statements
	A. Needs assessors ultimately are responsible for the success (or failure) of the needs assessment action plan. (circle one) <u>Strongly Agree</u> <u>Agree</u> <u>Disagree</u> <u>Strongly Disagree</u>
	B. Clients (those who receive program products/services) should be involved in every aspect of developing the needs assessment action plan. (circle one) <u>Strongly Agree</u> <u>Agree</u> <u>Disagree</u> <u>Strongly Disagree</u>
	C. Organizational policies that mandate change are essential to successfully implementing the needs assessment action plan. (circle one) <u>Strongly Agree</u> <u>Agree</u> <u>Disagree</u> <u>Strongly Disagree</u>
	D. The most critical element in fostering commitment to the needs assessment action plan is repeatedly communicating it by every means possible. (circle one) <u>Strongly Agree</u> <u>Agree</u> <u>Disagree</u> <u>Strongly Disagree</u>

Figure 3.3   Procedure 3: Choosing Corners

Procedure	Choosing Corners
Purpose	Promote positive interpersonal relations; reveal values and clarify assumptions
Time	10–15 minutes
Materials	• A list of questions (one or several) with four response options for each (post each response option in separate corners of the room; see samples below) • *Choosing Corners* handout (one per participant; see Figure 3.3a)

Directions	1. Present a question (or statement) and four alternative responses on a topic related to your needs assessment results; designate corners in the room where responses are posted.
	2. Instruct participants to choose the response that best matches personal proclivity; provide time for private thinking.
	3. Ask participants to move to the corner chosen; introduce and greet each other; and then exchange, compare, and contrast reasons.
	4. Facilitate whole-session sharing by systematically following up on each response option; move from corner to corner, asking several individuals within each to summarize key reasons for choices.
	5. Discuss what the responses/reasons reveal about the group/committee as a whole and implications for working together on postassessment tasks.
	6. If a question (or statement) has scaled response options (such as strongly agree, agree, disagree, strongly disagree; excellent, good, fair, poor; essential, useful, marginal, unnecessary), ask participants to use reasons revealed during whole-session sharing to revise the original statement to make it one that everyone can embrace (agree with, view as favorable, deem necessary).

Applications	Sample Questions/Statements
	Education: Which practice will most enhance student achievement?
	(Corners) 1. Standardized Testing 2. Professional Development 3. School Leadership 4. Parent Involvement
	Health: Public health initiatives should focus primarily on youth.
	(Corners) 1. Strongly Agree 2. Agree 3. Disagree 4. Strongly Disagree

Figure 3.3a   Choosing Corners (Handout)

Question	The corner I chose/my reasons why	The person I met (name)	His/her reasons for choosing this corner
Choosing Corners			
Directions:			
• Listen to the question and consider various responses posted in corners of the room.			
• Move to the corner that matches your personal response.			
• Greet and introduce yourself to one or two others in your corner.			
• Exchange reasons for choosing that corner. Compare and contrast reasons; notice similarities and differences.			
1.			
2.			
3.			
4.			
5.			

Source: © 1991 Laurie Stevahn.

Figure 3.4   Procedure 4: Making Metaphors

Procedure	Making Metaphors
Purpose	Promote positive interpersonal relations; reveal perceptions/reactions/insights
Time	5–10 minutes per metaphor
Materials	• A list of metaphor stems (open-ended sentence starters; see samples below) • A set of words, phrases, or illustrations to complete the metaphor stem (each participant selects one from the set; see samples below)
Directions	1. Present an open-ended metaphor stem; ask participants to complete it individually by either creating a response or selecting a response from a set of words, phrases, or illustrations. 2. Systematically ask participants to share their metaphors aloud; record and post responses. 3. Identify patterns, similar qualities, and/or unique outliers across the metaphor responses. 4. Discuss new insights revealed and their relevance to postassessment.
Applications	Sample Metaphor Stems • *A needs assessment that works is like a symphony because* . . . • *Implementing an action plan is like a roller coaster because* . . . • *Organizational change feels like . . . when* . . . • *Pitfalls during postassessment are like . . . because* . . . • *Successful needs assessors are most like* [provide a set of words from which participants select one such as *songbirds, giraffes, roosters, elephants, lizards, monkeys, eagles, armadillos, rabbits,* etc.] *. . . because* . . . • *Building commitment/support for the action plan happens best when* [provide a set of images such as art cards, postcards, photographs, illustrations, etc., from which participants each select one] *. . . because* . . .

Figure 3.5   Procedure 5: Cooperative Interviews

Procedure	Cooperative Interviews (See Chapter 4 for a detailed example.)
Purpose	Promote positive interpersonal relations; disclose perceptions/opinions/values
Time	10–20 minutes
Materials	• Interview topic/question (relevant to the needs assessment, useful for obtaining information, meaningful and thought provoking, linked to participants' personal background/experience, safe and nonthreatening, open-ended and answerable; see samples below) • Probing questions: Who? What? Where? When? Why? How? • *Interview Response Sheet* handout (one per team; see Figure 3.5a)
Directions	1. Arrange participants in teams of three. 2. Announce that the team goal is to gather input on the interview topic/question from all members; then synthesize and use it to address relevant issues. 3. Distribute the *Interview Response Sheet* (one per team). 4. Assign the following roles, one per teammate: (a) interviewer (seeks input), (b) responder (provides input), (c) recorder (writes input on the *Interview Response Sheet*). 5. Provide the interview topic/question and post probing questions; teammates rotate roles three times so that each will take a turn at interviewing, responding, and recording (use the same interview topic/question for each rotation). 6. Monitor time and instruct teams to rotate roles at designated intervals (e.g., every 3 minutes). 7. Instruct each team to look at its *Interview Response Sheet*. Identify similarities or common characteristics/qualities/themes threaded across the input. Notice outlier responses that provide insight to the topic. Make predictions and/or draw conclusions about the topic. 8. Discuss what this information means for successful postassessment.

Applications	Sample Interview Topics/Questions
	• Think of a time when you successfully made a positive change in your professional practice (or life). What was that change? Why did you make it? What influenced you to stick with it? What types of support were especially helpful in the transition?
	• What is your most cherished professional accomplishment? Why? When did it happen? Where? What was it about? Who was involved?
	• Is the needs assessment action plan making positive impact? How can you tell? What's different now? What still needs to be accomplished?

Figure 3.5a   Interview Response Sheet (Handout)

Interview Response Sheet	
Interview Topic/Question:	
Name	**Response**
Key Group Ideas *Similarities, Themes, Insights, Predictions, Conclusions*	

Source: © 1991 Laurie Stevahn.

Figure 3.6   Procedure 6: Roundtable/Roundrobin

Procedure	Roundtable/Roundrobin
Purpose	Promote positive interpersonal relations; share perceptions/ideas/reflections
Time	5–10 minutes
Materials	• Topic/Question/Issue (relevant to postassessment; see samples below) • *Roundtable Response Sheet* (one per team; see Figure 3.6a)
Directions	1. Arrange participants in teams of three or four. 2. Announce that the team goal is to gather information from all members on a topic relevant to postassessment. 3. Provide the topic/question/issue. 4. Distribute the *Roundtable Response Sheet* (one per team). 5. Roundtable occurs when the *Roundtable Response Sheet* rotates clockwise around the team; each member in turn writes and verbalizes one idea or insight. Roundrobin is the verbal-only variation; team members sequentially provide input orally. 6. If used for brainstorming, direct teams to conduct several clockwise rounds (e.g., members pass the *Roundtable Response Sheet* around the team three times). Teammates may provide new ideas or extend/elaborate previously presented ideas. 7. Input may be analyzed further by identifying common qualities, themes, or generalizations. 8. Discuss what the input means for successful postassessment.
Applications	Sample Topics/Questions/Issues • Which solution strategies do you find most compelling? Why? • What low-hanging fruit can be picked immediately to enact solution strategies in the needs assessment action plan? Brainstorm options. • How can we effectively communicate the needs assessment action plan to everyone in our program/department/organization? Brainstorm options. • What types of support/resources do people need to make changes specified in the needs assessment action plan? Why? • What evidence do you see that tells you the needs assessment action plan is working? • What (if any) new problems/difficulties/challenges/concerns have surfaced since taking steps to implement the needs assessment action plan?

	• Focus on one new concern/challenge that has surfaced. How might we address this issue? Generate ideas. • What have you learned from your involvement in this needs assessment? What should be remembered for future studies? Generate advice.

Figure 3.6a   Roundtable Response Sheet (Handout)

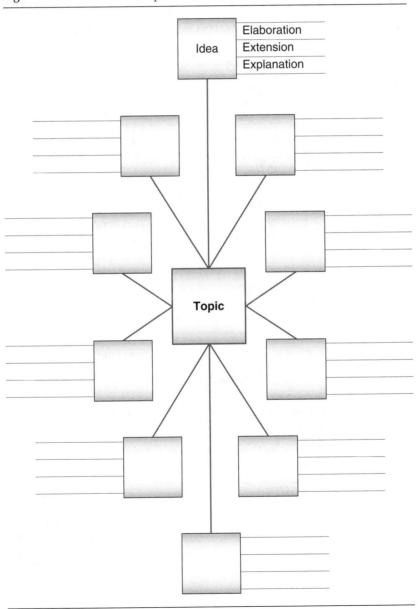

Figure 3.7   Procedure 7: Check-In/Tune-In

Procedure	Check-In/Tune-In
Purpose	Promote positive interpersonal relations; share reflections/ perceptions; summarize deliberations
Time	5–10 minutes
Materials	• Check-in question (relevant to postassessment; see samples below) • Chart paper (or alternative means to record/document input)
Directions	1. Use this procedure to open or close a meeting or during a session when transitioning from one topic/ activity to another. 2. Ask all participants a pertinent check-in question. Provide private think time. Emphasize the importance of keeping responses short. Model a sound-bite response. 3. Facilitate whole-session sharing by systematically asking each participant to provide a brief response; if desired, document contributions (using chart paper for further discussion, meeting minutes for future review, or electronic notes for needs assessment archives). 4. Summarize input and clarify implications for postassessment.
Applications	Sample Check-In Questions Opening Sessions • What is your current understanding of our purpose? • What experience do you bring to today's topic/task? • What word best describes your emotional reaction to the topic/task? • What points/ideas have you thought more about since our last session? Transitions Within Sessions • What is your biggest "Aha!"? What are you seeing more clearly now? • What is the most useful idea/information presented so far? • What is an important connection that you have made? • What question would you like answered before we move on?

	Closing Sessions • What did you especially value in this session? • What was most personally relevant to you in this session? • What was your most important lesson learned from this session? • What insight from this session will you carry away and act upon?

Figure 3.8   Procedure 8: Pluses/Wishes

Procedure	Pluses/Wishes
Purpose	Promote positive interpersonal relations; process tasks/ activities/interactions and summarize whole-group experiences/ dispositions
Time	5 minutes
Materials	• *Pluses/Wishes* handout (one per participant; see Figure 3.8a)
Directions	1. Use this procedure at the end of a meeting/session. 2. Distribute the *Pluses/Wishes* handout (one per participant). 3. Instruct all individuals to write in the "Pluses" column what they liked most about the session, found helpful, will especially remember, or can apply immediately. 4. Instruct all individuals to write in the "Wishes" column concerns, questions for clarification, requests, or suggestions for future sessions. 5. Collect the handouts and alert participants to the next scheduled meeting. 6. Analyze responses. 7. Start the next meeting by providing a summary of the pluses and wishes. 8. Respond to requests and suggestions whenever possible and appropriate.
Applications	Use this procedure consistently at every meeting/session. Systematically summarize and archive all input as a continuous source of evidence for documenting and evaluating the entire needs assessment for future endeavors.

Figure 3.8a   Pluses/Wishes (Handout)

Pluses Useful, Positive, Enjoyable	**Wishes** Concerns, Requests, Suggestions, Clarifications

Source: © 1991 Laurie Stevahn.

Figure 3.9   Procedure 9: PMI (Pluses/Minuses/Inquiries)/
PPP (Positives/Problems/Possibilities)

Procedure	PMI/PPP
Purpose	Promote positive interpersonal relations; process perceptions/experiences
Time	5–15 minutes
Materials	• *PMI* or *PPP* handout (one per participant; see Figure 3.9a)

Directions	1. Distribute the *PMI* or *PPP* handout (one per participant).
	2. Instruct all individuals to write responses corresponding to each category: PMI—<u>pluses</u>/advantages, <u>minuses</u>/disadvantages, and <u>inquiries</u>/questions relevant to the topic; PPP—<u>positives</u>/benefits, <u>problems</u>/negatives, and <u>possibilities</u>/suggestions for future action.
	3. Collect handouts and analyze responses (or facilitate whole-group analysis using *Procedure 12: Concept Formation*; see Figure 3.12).
	4. Summarize input and share findings.
	5. Respond to inquiries/questions and possibilities/suggestions whenever possible/appropriate.
Applications	Use this procedure at the end of meetings/tasks (like *Procedure 8: Pluses/Wishes*; see Figure 3.8) or to survey reactions to a specified topic, such as personal perceptions/experiences pertaining to a particular solution strategy.

Figure 3.9a PMI/PPP (Handouts)

PMI		PPP	
Pluses	**Minuses**	**Positives**	**Problems**
Inquiries		**Possibilities**	

Source: © 1991 Laurie Stevahn.

stand (or raise hands) to indicate the response category most applicable. The facilitator then asks participants to estimate response percentages across categories and venture generalizations about the entire group from that analysis. Items may include the following:

1. In what type of environment did you live as a child? Urban, suburban, rural?

2. Which of these cities most stirs your imagination or captures your heart, and why? London, Paris, Rome, Moscow, New York, Tokyo, others?

3. What do you like most about your/our own city or community? Its history, food, entertainment, diversity, architecture, celebrations, other characteristics?

4. How did you first learn about urban development? From a family member, from a friend, from an advertisement, in school, on the Internet, other?

5. How long have you worked in this urban development program? Fairly new, nearly a decade, nearly 2 decades, beyond?

6. Have you ever participated in a comprehensive needs assessment? Fully, somewhat, unsure?

7. Have you ever participated in creating an action plan? Yes, no, unsure?

When facilitating Procedures 1–9, select and adapt the content ahead of time to suit specific needs assessment contexts and situations. Notice, for example, that all of the items above were crafted specifically for the urban development program in which the assessment took place. Also decide whether to provide optional response choices (see examples in Figures 3.1–3.4) or open-ended questions/topics (see examples in Figures 3.5–3.9). Finally, remember that these procedures are not silly or frivolous icebreakers like those sometimes played at parties or other social gatherings. Although they can be fun and should be enjoyable— and some may derisively label them touchy-feely—ultimately they serve the serious purpose of helping people work together by engendering respect, compassion, liking, and trust.

Developing Shared Understandings

Although success relies on individual transformation during the needs assessment journey, personal growth and development isolated from others will do little to advance organizational change. Improvement ultimately occurs through the collective actions of individuals committed to making change happen. This necessitates conversations that cultivate shared understandings. Such conversations may focus on

1. *The mission, purpose, or goals of the organization or program*—and how needs assessment efforts advance those targets.

2. *The three-phase model of needs assessment*—its components, steps, and requirements.

3. *Alternatives/options for decision making*—any collection of items from which choices must be made such as a list of identified needs, possible solution strategies, or potential resources.

4. *The needs assessment action plan*—people not involved in action planning need to learn what it entails and understand what it requires.

5. *Data analysis*—effective decisions call for understanding and interpreting data, especially Phase II needs assessment data to determine needs and Phase III implementation data to assess progress.

Procedures 10–17 in Table 3.1 promote constructive conversations that foster shared understandings in the five areas noted above. Directions for facilitating these procedures appear in Figures 3.10–3.17. Notice that some invite participants to map, explain, interpret, or teach existing information, whereas others ask participants to provide input or generate information. Regardless, all of these activities involve individuals in discussions that require thoughtful reasoning, critical analysis, and social perspective taking—the very type of grappling required for making meaning of change.

Figure 3.10 Procedure 10: Jigsaw

Procedure	Jigsaw (See Chapter 4 for a detailed example.)
Purpose	Develop shared understandings
Time	1–2 hours (less time for simple/concise information divided into a few segments; more time for complex/voluminous information divided into numerous segments)

(Continued)

Figure 3.10 (Continued)

Materials	• Information packet (one packet per team; divide information into separate yet related segments like a jigsaw puzzle [color-code each segment if possible]; each packet contains one complete set of segments; arrange teams according to the number of segments in the packet—for example, arrange teams of three for a packet containing three segments, teams of four for four segments, teams of five for five segments, etc.; see illustration below)
Directions	1. Prepare the information packet prior to the meeting/session. 2. Arrange participants in teams according to the number of jigsaw segments in the packet (e.g., teams of three people for three segments). 3. Announce that the team goal is for all members to understand and use the entire body of information in the packet. Each member is responsible for a different segment of information, studies/learns it, and then presents it to the team. 4. Ask participants to silently read their own segment and note key points (allow appropriate time given the size/complexity of segments). 5. Instruct individuals to pair with someone from another team who has the same segment, compare key points, and then plan how to present that information (again, allow time given the size/complexity of segments). 6. Have individuals return to their original team and then in turn present segments. 7. Ask teams to apply the entire body of information to a postassessment task such as determining next steps, evaluating effectiveness of the action plan, or adjusting implementations. 8. Facilitate whole-session sharing by asking each team to report conclusions and then reach consensus on how to proceed.
Applications	**How well is Solution Strategy #1 working?** **Information:** ● = input from program administrators ■ = input from program service providers ◆ = input from program recipients **Original Teams:** ●■◆ ●■◆ ●■◆ ●■◆ ⬇ ⬆ **Expert Pairs:** ●● ●● ■■ ■■ ◆◆ ◆◆

Figure 3.11   Procedure 11: Graffiti/Carousel

Procedure	Graffiti/Carousel (See Chapter 4 for a detailed example.)
Purpose	Develop shared understandings
Time	50–60 minutes total (less time for few topics, more time for numerous topics) • Collect graffiti: 5–10 minutes. • Analyze/Synthesize graffiti: 45–50 minutes.
Materials	• Topics (different for each team; see samples below) • Graffiti sheets (chart paper, one per topic/team) • Sticky notes (e.g., Post-its—different color per topic/team) • Tables (one per team and/or wall space to post graffiti sheets)
Directions	1. Arrange teams; provide a separate topic and table for each (ideally three or four participants per team). 2. Announce that the team goal is to obtain input on a designated topic from all session participants; then analyze, synthesize, and report conclusions to the entire session. 3. Give each team one graffiti sheet (chart paper), each containing a different topic. 4. Provide each team with sticky notes such as Post-its (a different color per team). 5. Explain the graffiti activity: (a) All individuals silently/simultaneously write graffiti for 1–2 minutes on their team topic using sticky notes (one idea per sticky note, as many ideas as possible), (b) each team then passes its graffiti sheet clockwise to the next team (assign someone to carry the sheet to the next table), (c) all participants write graffiti on this new topic, (d) sheets continue to rotate clockwise until each team's original topic returns home, and (e) then teams analyze and synthesize the graffiti on the topic/sheet by grouping similar items/ideas (see *Procedure 12: Concept Formation*, Figure 3.12).
Applications	**Sample Topics** Topic 1: I feel supported in my work when … Topic 2: I feel frustrated in my work when … Topic 3: I will make change when … Topic 4: The action plan will work if … Topic 5: Ways to communicate the plan are … Topic 6: Helpful resources for the plan are …

Figure 3.12   Procedure 12: Concept Formation

Procedure	Concept Formation (See Chapter 4 for a detailed example.)			
Purpose	Develop shared understandings			
Time	30–60 minutes			
Materials	• Data sets (one set per team containing 20–50 items, each written on a separate card, paper strip, or sticky note; see sample below)			
Directions	1. Arrange participants in teams of two, three, or four. 2. Announce that the team goal is to summarize a set of data using qualitative analysis. 3. Give each team one data set containing a collection of items. 4. Instruct teams to group/categorize/cluster items that are alike (i.e., items with similar defining attributes). 5. Assign a specific role to each teammate if helpful, for example: (a) card mover—clusters cards based on team consensus; (b) scribe—takes notes on team discussion/ reasoning; (c) theme recorder—writes agreed-upon labels/names for clusters based on defining attributes; and (d) time keeper—keeps team on task and alerts teammates to time deadlines. 6. Label or name each group/category/cluster (create a label/name that reflects the underlying attribute among items in the cluster; each cluster represents a major theme). 7. Facilitate whole-session sharing by asking each team to present and post themes; identify repeated themes across teams; describe relationships/connections among themes. 8. Apply the major themes to postassessment concerns/ issues/decisions.			
Applications	Sample Data Set: Helpful Resources	Sample Clusters/Themes		
		Training	Technology	Data Management
	1. Assistance with technology 2. Clerks to file/organize findings 3. Training for new procedures 4. Set up a Web site for clients	3. 8. 9.	1. 4. 10.	2. 5. 6. 7. 11.

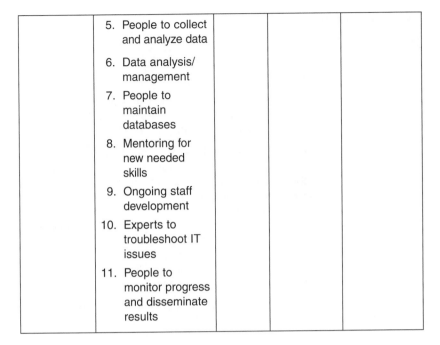

	5. People to collect and analyze data			
	6. Data analysis/ management			
	7. People to maintain databases			
	8. Mentoring for new needed skills			
	9. Ongoing staff development			
	10. Experts to troubleshoot IT issues			
	11. People to monitor progress and disseminate results			

Figure 3.13 Procedure 13: Concept Mapping/Mind Mapping

Procedure	Concept Mapping/Mind Mapping
Purpose	Develop shared understandings
Time	45–60 minutes
Materials	• Topic (or information sheet; see samples below) • Sample concept map or mind map (see Figure 3.13a) • Chart paper (one sheet per team) • Felt markers (a variety of colors, one set per team)
Directions	1. Arrange participants in teams of three or four. 2. Announce that the team goal is to create a concept map or mind map for a particular topic (or body of information). Show a sample map (Figure 3.13a). 3. Give each team one sheet of chart paper and a set of felt markers.

Figure 3.13 (Continued)

	4. Present the topic (or distribute an information sheet on the topic).
	5. Instruct teams to create a map that depicts or illustrates various dimensions/aspects of the topic and interconnections among them.
	6. Explain how to create a map: (a) Write the topic in the center of the chart paper; (b) add relevant ideas, aspects, dimensions, examples, and details; (c) draw lines/arrows from the central topic to each added item; (d) indicate connections/relationships among items; (e) use different colors to enhance meaning; and (f) illustrate mind maps by drawing a symbol or visual for each item. The final concept map looks like a word web; the final mind map also contains symbols/illustrations.
	7. Assign a specific role to each teammate if helpful (such as materials manager, writer, illustrator, and time keeper).
	8. Facilitate whole-session sharing by asking each team to present its map. Identify similarities/differences across maps.
	9. Apply mind maps to postassessment concerns/issues/decisions.
	10. Note: Themes relevant to a central topic, like those that emerge from *Procedure 12: Concept Formation* (Figure 3.12), can be used to create a map. Maps often are useful for presenting analyzed data sets.
Applications	Sample Topics • Practical solution strategies for dealing with an identified need • Possible stakeholder groups/individuals to involve in action planning • Helpful resources for implementing the action plan • Potential barriers to implementing the action plan • Ways to monitor implementation progress • Lessons learned from the overall needs assessment

Figure 3.13a   Sample Maps

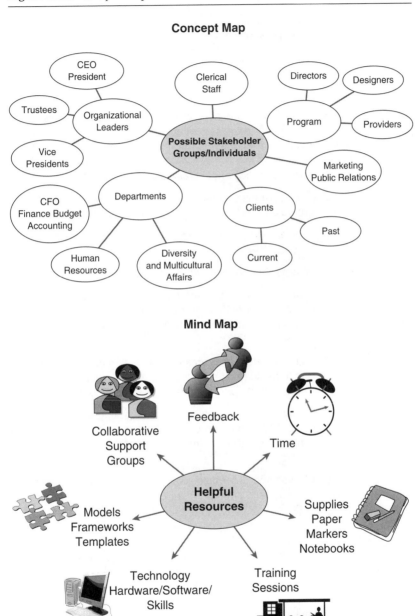

Figure 3.14   Procedure 14: Force Field Analysis

Procedure	Force Field Analysis
Purpose	Prioritize and finalize decisions
Time	30–60 minutes
Materials	• Set of factors (enabling or blocking success/progress; one set per team; see samples below) • *Force Field Analysis* handout (see Figure 3.14a)
Directions	1. Arrange participants in teams of two or three. 2. Announce that the team goal is to determine factors that promote/enable and impede/block success or progress. 3. Give each team one *Force Field Analysis* handout (Figure 3.14a). 4. Give each team one set of factors. 5. Instruct teams to sort the factors into two categories: enabling factors (left column) and blocking factors (right column); note that teams may add factors of their own to the list. 6. If appropriate, ask teams to rank factors in each column from most to least enabling or blocking by using *Procedure 21: Cooperative Rank Order* (Figure 3.21). 7. Facilitate whole-session sharing by asking each team to present and post *Force Field Analysis* charts; compare, contrast, and discuss implications for the needs assessment. 8. Discuss and determine ways to remove impeding factors and maintain, strengthen, or extend promotive factors.

Applications	Sample Set of Factors		
	A. Clear goals	D. Lack of ongoing training	G. Isolated staff
	B. Lack of collaboration	E. Outdated technology	H. Leaders not visible
	C. Timely directives	F. Policy for staff support	I. Low morale

Figure 3.14a   Force Field Analysis (Handout)

Force Field Analysis	
Promotive Factors → (Enable, Drive, Support Success)	← **Impeding Factors** (Block, Inhibit, Obstruct Success)

Source: © 2000 Laurie Stevahn.

Figure 3.15   Procedure 15: Fishbone Analysis

Procedure	Fishbone Analysis
Purpose	Prioritize and finalize decisions
Time	45–60 minutes
Materials	• Targeted problem/outcome/effect (see samples below) • Major causes or influencing factors (see samples below) • *Fishbone Analysis* charts (see Figure 3.15a) • Chart paper (one sheet per team) • Felt markers (one marker per team)
Directions	1. Arrange people in teams of two, three, or four. 2. Announce that the team goal is to determine causes of a problem (or factors that influence an outcome). The template in Figure 3.15a includes the most common causes, which may be adapted. The final analysis looks like a fish skeleton.

(Continued)

Figure 3.15 (Continued)

	3. Display the sample *Fishbone Analysis* chart and explain how to create it: (a) Draw a horizontal line pointing to the targeted problem/outcome/effect recorded at the right, (b) draw additional branching lines above and below that each point to a major cause/factor, and (c) identify specifics for each cause/factor relevant to the organization/program/needs assessment context.
	4. Distribute one sheet of chart paper and one felt marker to each team.
	5. Specify the problem/outcome and the major causes/factors.
	6. Instruct teams to create a fishbone chart.
	7. Facilitate whole-session sharing by asking teams to present and post fishbone charts; compare, contrast, and identify repeated patterns across charts (repetition suggests root causes/factors); and discuss implications for the needs assessment.
	8. Apply the results to postassessment concerns/issues/decisions.
	9. Note: Adaptations include (a) whole-session creation of one fishbone chart in which one recorder captures input from everyone or (b) whole-session jigsaw using *Procedure 10: Jigsaw* (Figure 3.10) in which each team works on a separate and different cause/factor and then contributes that piece to the whole.
Applications	Sample Problems/Outcomes and Causes/Factors

Problem/Outcome	Causes/Factors
• Staff training	Policies, Person-Power, Communications, Resources/Materials, Facilities
• Commitment to the action plan	Policies, Person-Power, Communications, Resources/Materials, Facilities

Figure 3.15a   Fishbone Analysis Charts

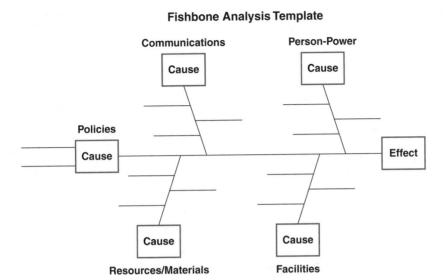

Fishbone Analysis Template

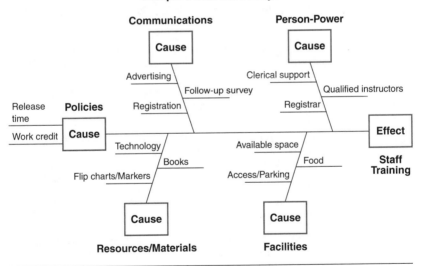

Sample Fishbone Analysis Chart

Source: © 2005 Laurie Stevahn & Jean A. King [Sample chart only].

Figure 3.16   Procedure 16: What? So What? Now What?

Procedure	What? So What? Now What?
Purpose	Develop shared understandings
Time	30–60 minutes
Materials	• Needs assessment plans/information/results (one set per team; see sample scenarios below) • *What? So What? Now What?* handout (one per team; see Figure 3.16a)
Directions	1. Arrange participants in teams of three. 2. Announce that the team goal is to review and understand information, identify implications for practice, and then determine appropriate actions. 3. Distribute needs assessment plans/information/results (one set per team). 4. Provide time for individuals to silently read/review the information and highlight key points/insights. 5. Distribute the *What? So What? Now What?* handout (one per team). 6. Instruct teammates to take turns facilitating and recording team discussion on each component: (a) The first person facilitates/records discussion on *What?* (What is the information?—literally describe it); (b) the second person facilitates/records discussion on *So What?* (So what does the information imply or mean for practice?); and (c) the third person facilitates/records discussion on *Now What?* (Now what specific actions can/should be taken to address the implications for practice?). 7. Facilitate whole-session sharing by asking each team to present its thinking; compile all input on a master chart. 8. Conduct a whole-session discussion on the master chart; reach agreement on which courses of action to pursue. 9. Note: Actions specified under *Now What?* (third column) can be ranked using *Procedure 21: Cooperative Rank Order* (Figure 3.21) or mapped using *Procedure 13: Concept Mapping/Mind Mapping* (Figure 3.13).

Applications	Sample Scenarios
	• Provide possible solution strategies to the NAC (one per small group)
	• Provide the action plan (developed by the NAC) to program providers
	• Provide information on communicating the action plan to organizational leaders
	• Provide information describing organizational system supports to leaders responsible for communicating plans to staff
	• Provide a set of analyzed data (collected to monitor implementation progress) to the NAC

Figure 3.16a   What? So What? Now What? (Handout)

What?	So What?	Now What?
Descriptions	Implications	Actions

Source: © 1998 Laurie Stevahn.

Figure 3.17   Procedure 17: Rubric Reflections

Procedure	Rubric Reflections
Purpose	Develop shared understandings
Time	30–60 minutes (depending on amount of needs assessment information and length of rubric)
Materials	• Implementation information (one per participant; see samples below) • *Rubric* handout (one per participant; see Figure 3.17a)
Directions	1. Prior to facilitating this procedure, adapt the *Rubric* (Figure 3.17a) by including only those factors applicable to the information provided (or create/use a different applicable rubric). 2. Distribute implementation information to all participants. 3. Distribute the *Rubric* handout to all participants. 4. Explain and demonstrate how to apply the *Rubric* to the information (e.g., model how to apply the first factor). 5. Ask participants to silently read/review the information and individually apply the rubric to evaluate appropriate factors. 6. Arrange participants in teams of three or four. 7. Instruct teammates to share/compare/contrast their rubric evaluations and provide rationales for personal ratings (similar ratings indicate agreement; diverse ratings indicate disagreement). 8. Instruct teams to discuss ratings, perceptions, and implications for future postassessment steps/tasks/activities. 9. Facilitate whole-session sharing by asking each team to present its analysis; then agree on how to proceed.
Applications	Sample Implementation Information • The needs assessment action plan (or segments of it) • Strategies to communicate/disseminate the action plan • Information on organizational/program structure (or support systems) • Information on organizational/program resources • Feedback on how the action plan is perceived by stakeholders • Analyzed data collected to monitor implementation progress • Any substantive information that can be assessed/judged

Figure 3.17a   Rubric (Handout)

<table>
<tr><td colspan="2" align="center">**Rubric**</td></tr>
<tr><td colspan="2">**Directions:**
- Silently read the information provided.
- Individually apply the rubric to the information.
- Share your judgments with others and explain your reasoning.
- Compare and contrast similar and different judgments and rationales.
- Try to reach consensus on judgments that differ.
- Look across all factors/judgments to summarize overall conclusions about the information.</td></tr>
<tr><td>**Factor**</td><td align="center">**Assessment**</td></tr>
<tr><td>**1. Tone/Attitude**</td><td>Negative **1 2 3 4 5 6 7** Positive
Reasons:</td></tr>
<tr><td>**2. Environment/ Climate**</td><td>Negative **1 2 3 4 5 6 7** Positive
Reasons:</td></tr>
<tr><td>**3. Motivation**</td><td>Flat **1 2 3 4 5 6 7** Enthusiastic
Reasons:</td></tr>
<tr><td>**4. Commitment**</td><td>Weak **1 2 3 4 5 6 7** Strong
Reasons:</td></tr>
<tr><td>**5. Strategies/ Directives**</td><td>Unclear **1 2 3 4 5 6 7** Clear
Reasons:</td></tr>
<tr><td>**6. Communications**</td><td>Unclear **1 2 3 4 5 6 7** Clear
Reasons:</td></tr>
<tr><td>**7. Skills**</td><td>Nonexistent **1 2 3 4 5 6 7** Extensive
Reasons:</td></tr>
<tr><td>**8. Support**</td><td>Nonexistent **1 2 3 4 5 6 7** Extensive
Reasons:</td></tr>
<tr><td>**10. Barriers**</td><td>Nonexistent **1 2 3 4 5 6 7** Extensive
Reasons:</td></tr>
<tr><td>**11. Progress**</td><td>Slow **1 2 3 4 5 6 7** Rapid
Reasons:</td></tr>
<tr><td>**12. Change**</td><td>Unsuccessful **1 2 3 4 5 6 7** Successful
Reasons:</td></tr>
</table>

Source: © 2000 Laurie Stevahn.

Procedures 10–17 are especially useful in postassessment when people must understand alternatives or options prior to decision making. In fact, creating the action plan primarily consists of choosing among alternatives—hence, the importance of understanding their substance, implications, and requirements. Consider, for example, the director of a senior center serving a large and culturally diverse geographic population in a major metropolitan area. Working with an external evaluator, the director is conducting a needs assessment of the center's largest program, which serves African American, Hispanic, and East African residents. The most critical need has been targeted, and five possible solution strategies have been identified. Today, the director and evaluator are meeting with the NAC to help members understand the five alternative strategies, only one or two of which can be implemented due to limited resources. *Procedure 10: Jigsaw* (Figure 3.10) will be used to engage participants in critically examining the five options. The activity starts by arranging teams, each comprising five people. Each team receives one set of solution strategy sheets, numbered 1 through 5. Teammates also number themselves 1 through 5, each individually responsible for the sheet that corresponds to his or her exclusive number. Individuals silently read their material and then find another person from a different team who also is responsible for that same material. This reorganization results in partnerships, each focused on a different and exclusive strategy, such as the Strategy 1 pair, Strategy 2 pair, Strategy 3 pair, and so on. These content-alike pairs discuss their information, outline key points, and then prepare how best to present those points once they return to their original teams of five. This interactive process enables everyone to better understand all five options before making final choices.

Procedures 10–17 also are particularly useful for helping people collectively comprehend how well the needs assessment action plan is working. Any effective postassessment effort must monitor progress, the heart of which involves collecting and making sense of implementation data. Consider, for example, a needs assessor working in a suburban neighborhood health clinic who has interviewed staff and patients about their experiences with the new practices set forth in the action plan. The assessor now decides to present the analyzed data to the steering committee guiding the implementation. *Procedure 16: What? So What? Now What?* (Figure 3.16) will be used to engage participants in making sense of the data. Everyone receives the handout outlining the structure of the discussion (Figure 3.16a).

- First, participants discuss/describe the analysis: *What* do the data reveal about how respondents perceive their experiences with the new practices?
- Next, participants discuss/infer implications: *So what* does this mean for continuing or modifying those practices?
- Finally, participants consider/plan next steps: *Now what* do we do? What adjustments should be made? What successes should be publicized and celebrated?

Such discussions promote greater understanding of solution strategies in practice and provide opportunities to fine-tune the action plan when warranted.

Of course, adapt Procedures 10–17 as required by the unique circumstances, settings, and contexts of your situation. Also consider the nature of the information that you wish people to comprehend (quantitative, qualitative, simple, complex, technical, etc.), amount (large or small), and number of individuals involved (few or numerous). Some procedures are especially useful for fostering shared understandings when large amounts of information can be subdivided among many committee participants (e.g., *Procedure 10: Jigsaw*), whereas others may be better for small committees (three to five people) or when information is best addressed holistically (e.g., *Procedure 16: What? So What? Now What?*).

Finally, remember that concerns, fears, and anxieties surface when people face change. Individually and collectively struggling with these issues enables people to grow in ways that support meaningful transformation. The good news is that Procedures 10–17 shepherd people through the process. As participants work together to make sense of information for planning and implementing action, they are also simultaneously clarifying their own uncertainties about change.

Prioritizing and Finalizing Decisions

Sound decisions ground postassessment, as emphasized in Table 1.3. Steps 11 and 12 focus on decisions for the action plan; Steps 13 and 14 focus on decisions about its implementation and effectiveness. A useful plan will designate which initiatives to pursue first, tasks to be completed, who will be involved, how resources will be allocated or shifted to get the job done, methods for tracking and reporting progress, and a reasonable timeline for doing so (see Chapter 2).

Procedures 18–24 in Table 3.1 engage participants in collectively setting priorities and making decisions. Directions for facilitating these procedures appear in Figures 3.18–3.24. Procedures 18–20 are quick and simple and require few materials. For example, *Procedure 18: Fist to Five* (Figure 3.18) can be used on the spot to determine which solution strategies people view as most urgent, feasible, or necessary. The facilitator simply presents an option and then asks participants to respond on a scale from 0 to 5 (lowest to highest priority) by showing zero to five fingers. Systematically seeking input in this way across a list of options quickly reveals priorities. *Procedure 19: Dot Voting* (Figure 3.19) can also be used easily and with little preparation. For example, when the NAC must decide how best to communicate the action plan to program staff and clients, the facilitator posts 10 options on chart paper and then gives each member three dots to vote for three different alternatives; those receiving the most votes are the options pursued.

Figure 3.18   Procedure 18: Fist to Five

Procedure	Fist to Five
Purpose	Prioritize and finalize decisions; assess progress; promote positive interpersonal relationships
Time	5–10 minutes (depending on the number of items considered)
Materials	• List of items (to be rated/prioritized; see samples below)
Directions	1. Present a list of items.
	2. Ask participants to rate/prioritize each item on a scale from 0 to 5 (low represented by a fist to high represented by five fingers). Specify what the low/fist to high/five scale indicates, such as from least to most important, needed, essential, effective, representative, knowledgeable, useful, doable, preferred, valued, etc.
	3. Ask participants to estimate an average for each item by looking across everyone's ratings; document/record results.
	4. Review ratings across the entire list of items; discuss implications and determine priorities.
	5. Note: This procedure allows quick assessment of priorities but requires public disclosure, which eliminates confidentiality.

Applications	Sample Items
	Action Plan Components (*undesirable/unworkable* to *highly desirable/workable*) • Solution Strategy 1, 2, 3, etc. (consider each separately in turn) • Communicating the action plan electronically • Monitoring progress by surveying clients • Monitoring progress by interviewing staff **Needs Assessment Characteristics** (*none* to *lots*) • Knowledge of organizational change • Expertise in qualitative analysis • Expertise in quantitative analysis • Prior experience in action planning • Familiarity with managing databases **Personal Characteristics** (*that's not me* to *that's totally me*) • Always dreamed of working in this profession/discipline • Came to this profession/discipline by accident • Have worked in every department in the organization

Figure 3.19   Procedure 19: Dot Voting

Procedure	Dot Voting
Purpose	Prioritize and finalize decisions; assess progress
Time	10–20 minutes (depending on number of items and length of debriefing)
Materials	• Items/Alternatives (to prioritize/choose; post each on a separate chart sheet; see samples below) • Sticky dots, stickers, or sticky notes (e.g., Post-its)
Directions	1. Post items/alternatives on the wall (one per chart sheet). 2. Provide each participant with an equal number of sticky dots (more if many alternatives exist, less if fewer alternatives exist). 3. Instruct participants to indicate which items/alternatives are most desired (or preferred, important, valued, attainable, feasible, etc.) by placing dots on the corresponding chart sheets.

(Continued)

Figure 3.19 (Continued)

	4. Explain the rules for voting before asking people to make choices (especially when individuals have multiple dots). For example, indicate whether all or several dots can be devoted to a single item/alternative or whether each dot must be devoted to different items/alternatives. 5. Tally totals for each option; record results on each chart sheet. 6. Apply the results (priorities/decisions) to postassessment.
Applications	Sample Items/Alternatives Item A = Conduct telephone interviews Item B = Conduct focus group sessions Item C = Administer electronic surveys

Item A	Item B	Item C
○ ○ ○ ○ ○ ○ ○ ○	○ ○ ○ ○ ○ ○ ○ ○ ○ ○ ○ ○ ○ ○ ○ ○	○ ○ ○ ○ ○ ○ ○ ○ ○ ○ ○

Figure 3.20   Procedure 20: Bar Graphs

Procedure	Bar Graphs
Purpose	Prioritize and finalize decisions
Time	10–20 minutes (depending on number of items and length of debriefing)
Materials	• Items/Alternatives (to prioritize/choose/rank; see samples below) • Large bar graph (chart paper showing items/alternatives on one axis; see sample below) • Sticky notes, sticky dots, or stickers (uniform in size/shape)
Directions	1. Post the bar graph on the wall (chart paper). 2. Give each participant one sticky note (or several, equal in number and uniform in size/shape).

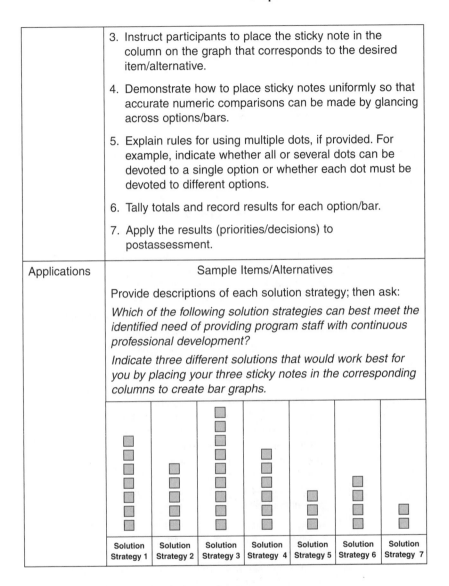

3. Instruct participants to place the sticky note in the column on the graph that corresponds to the desired item/alternative.

4. Demonstrate how to place sticky notes uniformly so that accurate numeric comparisons can be made by glancing across options/bars.

5. Explain rules for using multiple dots, if provided. For example, indicate whether all or several dots can be devoted to a single option or whether each dot must be devoted to different options.

6. Tally totals and record results for each option/bar.

7. Apply the results (priorities/decisions) to postassessment.

Applications	Sample Items/Alternatives

Provide descriptions of each solution strategy; then ask:

Which of the following solution strategies can best meet the identified need of providing program staff with continuous professional development?

Indicate three different solutions that would work best for you by placing your three sticky notes in the corresponding columns to create bar graphs.

Solution Strategy 1	Solution Strategy 2	Solution Strategy 3	Solution Strategy 4	Solution Strategy 5	Solution Strategy 6	Solution Strategy 7

Procedures 21–24 are more elaborate, time consuming, and materials intensive, demanding critical discourse and sustained focus to reach consensus on final choices. For example, *Procedure 21: Cooperative Rank Order* (Figure 3.21) can be used to engage the NAC in rigorous reflection and decision making. The facilitator first arranges and provides each small group with one set of options, each alternative written on a separate card or paper strip. Group members rank the options from most strategic to least strategic, recording issues that emerge

during discussion and rationales used to determine the final rank. The NAC finalizes choices by comparing and discussing rankings and rationales across groups, mutually adopting those strategies consistently ranked highest.

Figure 3.21   Procedure 21: Cooperative Rank Order

Procedure	Cooperative Rank Order
Purpose	Prioritize and finalize decisions
Time	60 minutes (more or less time depending on the number of items in the set)
Materials	• Set of items (to rank/order/sequence; one set per team; each set contains 6–12 items, each written on a separate card or paper strip; see sample below)
Directions	1. Arrange participants in teams of two, three, or four. 2. The team goal is to reach consensus on a rank, order, or sequence for a collection of items. 3. Give each team one set of items. 4. Instruct teams to rank the items according to an established criterion (such as importance, desirability, feasibility, level of difficulty, amount of training required, probable benefits, likelihood of success, etc.). Place cards or paper strips in an order that reflects "most to least" using the criterion specified. Items that describe actions or behaviors can be sequenced according to which should come first, second, third, and so on, to best accomplish a targeted goal. 5. Assign a specific role to each teammate if helpful, for example: (a) card mover—arranges cards in order based on team consensus, (b) scribe—takes notes on team discussion/reasoning, (c) time keeper—keeps team on task and alerts teammates to time deadlines, and (d) reporter—presents the team's final product to the entire session. 6. Facilitate whole-session sharing by asking each team to present and post rankings; identify which items repeatedly are ranked highest or lowest across teams and discuss implications for the needs assessment. 7. Apply the results to postassessment concerns/issues/decisions.

Applications	Sample Set of Items
	Identified Need: Increase knowledge of and commitment to the organization's mission. *Rank-order the following set of solution strategies from most to least feasible.* *Next, sequence the same set from greatest to least potential for positive impact.*

	A. Post the mission in every space.	D. Distribute mission bookmarks.
	B. Designate a monthly mission day.	E. State mission on all documents.
	C. Staff shares ways to live mission.	F. Revisit mission at each meeting.

Figure 3.22   Procedure 22: Multi-Attribute Consensus Reaching (MACR)

Procedure	MACR
Purpose	Prioritize and finalize decisions
Time	1–2 hours (depending on the number of factors)
Materials	• Factors (see samples below) • *Essential Factors* handout (one per participant; see Figure 3.22a) • Computer/Software (to calculate mean and range for each rating) • Projection system (to display results immediately)
Directions	1. Arrange seats in a circle (around the table or room). 2. Set up the computer/software and projection system. 3. The whole-session goal is to determine which factors are essential. 4. Distribute the *Essential Factors* handout (one per participant).

(Continued)

Figure 3.22 (Continued)

	5. Instruct participants to silently/independently rate each factor using the scale provided; complete the entire handout.
	6. Systematically facilitate whole-session sharing: (a) Start with the first factor, (b) participants in turn share ratings aloud, (c) enter ratings into the computer database, (d) calculate the mean and range, (e) display results using the projection system, (f) participants discuss personal ratings and rationales, (g) after discussion participants can revise ratings, (h) repeat this process for each factor, and (i) participants submit handouts showing initial and revised ratings at the end of the session.
	7. Interpret results: (a) Small variance/range indicates agreement (e.g., zero variance indicates 100% agreement); (b) the mean indicates where on the scale agreement exists (e.g., a large mean indicates that the factor is essential, and a small mean indicates that the factor is not essential); and (c) large variance/range indicates disagreement that the factor is essential (regardless of the mean).
	8. Use results to finalize priorities/decisions on essential factors.

Applications	Sample Factors	
	Classification	**Factors**
	■ Identified needs →	Staff training, updated technology, client input
	■ Solution strategies for staff training →	Off-site institutes, on-site workshops, on-the-job training, weekly skill demonstrations, online courses
	■ Criteria for evaluating solution strategies →	Cost, convenience, best practice, quick implementation, learning styles

Figure 3.22a   Essential Factors (Handout)

Essential Factors

Directions:
- Independently complete this sheet.
- Use the scale to rate the importance/feasibility of each factor.
- Write the number that represents your rating (from 0 = least to 6 = most).
- Record your <u>Initial Rating</u> in the corresponding column.
- After whole-session discussion, record a <u>Revised Rating</u> if warranted.

Rating Scale

Less Important/Feasible	Somewhat Important/Feasible	More Important/Feasible

```
 0     1     2     3     4     5     6
```

Factors	Initial Rating	**Revised Rating** (Write SAME if no change.)
Factor 1: _____ <u>Rationale:</u>		
Factor 2: _____ <u>Rationale:</u>		
Factor 3: _____ <u>Rationale:</u>		
Factor 4: _____ <u>Rationale:</u>		
Factor 5: _____ <u>Rationale:</u>		
Factor 6: _____ <u>Rationale:</u>		

Figure 3.23   Procedure 23: Delphi Method/Nominal Group Technique

Procedure	Delphi Method/Nominal Group Technique	
Purpose	Prioritize and finalize decisions	
Time	1–2 hours (or across several meeting sessions)	
Materials	Issue/Topic/Problem (for decision making; see samples below) Chart paper and felt markers (to record/document whole-session input)	
Directions	Delphi Method	Nominal Group Technique
	1. Present the issue/topic/problem.	1. Present the issue/topic/problem.
	2. Ask participants privately to write ideas/opinions/solutions without discussion.	2. Ask participants privately to write ideas/opinions/solutions without discussion.
	3. Instruct participants to submit their ideas anonymously.	3. Instruct participants to present their ideas to everyone; record and post on a master chart.
	4. Summarize all input; provide the summary to participants.	4. Facilitate whole-session discussion to clarify all ideas.
	5. Ask participants to review the summary without discussion; then revise earlier ideas/opinions/solutions if warranted by writing and submitting additional input anonymously.	5. Ask each participant individually to rank numerically the top five ideas (rate the first as 1, the second as 2, the third as 3, etc.).
	6. Repeat this process until ideas/opinions/solutions stabilize; these become the highest priorities or final decisions.	6. Average the ratings for each idea and sequence the averages from low to high; the idea with the lowest average is the highest priority or final decision.

Applications	Sample Issues/Topics/Problems	
	Issue/Topic/Problem	**Question/Decision**
	■ Funding permits only one → solution strategy to be enacted.	Which solution strategy should we implement?
	■ Clients are confused about → new policies/practices.	How can we improve communication with clients to eliminate confusion?
	■ Service providers need → additional skills to enact the action plan.	How can we equip service providers with required skills?

Figure 3.24   Procedure 24: Constructive Controversy

Procedure	Constructive Controversy
Purpose	Prioritize and finalize decisions
Time	2 hours (or across several meeting sessions if appropriate)
Materials	• Controversy issue and specified advocacy positions (see sample below) • *Background Information* handout (prepare/provide if appropriate)
Directions	1. Arrange participants in teams of four and specify the controversy issue. 2. The team goal is to use the controversy process to mutually agree on the best-reasoned solution to a specified issue. 3. Post and explain the controversy process (prepare, present, discuss, reverse, synthesize; see Johnson & Johnson, 2007): (a) Teams of four subdivide into pairs; (b) each pair advocates an alternative position on a specified issue (e.g., pro/con, for/against, yes/no, favor/oppose); and (c) pairs <u>prepare</u> the best case possible for their assigned position (using *Background Information* if provided), <u>present</u> each case in turn, openly <u>discuss</u> by refuting and rebutting points, <u>reverse</u> perspectives by arguing the other side, and then drop all advocacy to jointly <u>synthesize</u> a solution to the issue.

Figure 3.24 (Continued)

	4. Synthesizing evidence often leads to reframing the original issue, which opens new possibilities for creative solutions. Provide an example (like the sample below). 5. Note: Whole-session controversy involves dividing all participants into two large advocacy groups that prepare their cases, present to everyone, openly discuss points, reverse positions, and then synthesize a solution.		
Applications	Sample Controversy Issue and Advocacy Positions		

Original Issue	Advocacy Positions	
	YES	**NO**
Are focus group data credible?	• Individuals respond directly • Private written input prior to discussion reduces bias • More people can give input • Used often across disciplines • Expert facilitators hired	• Group discussion biases individual responding • Samples are too small to generalize findings • Few topics are discussed • Internal facilitators not trained

Reframed Issue	Final Synthesized Solution
What constitutes credible actionable data?	Data that are valid and reliable for a specified purpose are credible and actionable. Regardless of methods, collect data in ways that enhance validity and reliability for decisions/actions.

Before selecting Procedures 18–24 for prioritizing and finalizing group decisions, consider the nature and substance of the choices, the value of in-depth discussion, available time, and skills necessary for participation. Which decisions can be made quickly and without much discussion in your needs assessment context? Which will require extended discussion and deliberation? Do participants possess the skills demanded by the various procedures, or will teaching and modeling various skills be important for success? Can the procedures deemed most promising be implemented adequately within established schedules and timelines? Make necessary adjustments and adaptations accordingly.

Finally, remember the value of inclusive decision making; it tends to enhance personal commitment to implementation. Those who create the needs assessment action plan will likely dedicate themselves to living it. Typologies that present methods for decision making underscore this point. For example, consider the continuum of methods shown in Table 3.3. They range from unilateral decision making by designated leaders to mutual decision making by all stakeholders.

Table 3.3   Methods for Decision Making

Methods	Advantages	Disadvantages
1. *Authority Decision Without Input* (leader/authority decides without stakeholder input or discussion)	Useful when time is limited; especially appropriate for administrative decisions in which stakeholders have no interest or expertise.	Stakeholder input not sought or used in decision making; does not develop commitment to implement decisions.
2. *Expert Decision* (expert decides without stakeholder input or discussion)	Useful when an expert with pertinent superior knowledge exists, especially when leaders/authorities and stakeholders deem the expert legitimate and credible.	Difficult to know who is expert; stakeholder input not sought or used in decision making; does not develop commitment to implement decisions.
3. *Average Opinion Decision* (decisions made by individually surveying stakeholders, then averaging their opinions)	Stakeholders provide input; prominent themes/preferences identified; useful for simple or routine decisions.	Little (if any) interaction among stakeholders; does not develop commitment to implement decisions.

(Continued)

Table 3.3 (Continued)

Methods	Advantages	Disadvantages
4. *Authority Decision After Input* (leader/authority decides after seeking input and discussion from stakeholders)	Stakeholders provide input; may broaden perspectives of the leader who decides.	Stakeholders may tell the leader only what he/she wishes to hear; the leader may ignore stakeholder input; does not develop commitment to implement decisions.
5. *Minority Decision* (representatives decide)	Selected decision makers represent stakeholders; useful when everyone cannot feasibly participate in decision making (such as in large organizations or multisite situations).	Selected decision makers may not seek or use stakeholder input, relay information, or represent constituents adequately; does not foster widespread commitment to implement decisions.
6. *Majority Decision* (majority decides by voting)	Involves all stakeholders in decision making through voting; useful when time is short; winners more committed to implement decisions than losers.	Little (if any) interpersonal interaction among stakeholders; may alienate losers and thereby damage future working relations.
7. *Consensus Decision* (stakeholders decide by consensus)	Stakeholders provide input and mutually reach agreement; tends to produce innovative, creative, and high-quality decisions; develops commitment to implement the decision.	Time intensive; requires sophisticated interpersonal skills; demands sustained focus and energy.

From Johnson & Johnson, JOINING TOGETHER, "Decision-Making Methods," pp. 283–284, © 2009. Reproduced by permission of Pearson Education, Inc.

The advantages and disadvantages of these various methods consistently indicate that involvement tends to increase as well as broaden commitment. These methods also remind us that not all decisions should (or can) be made by all stakeholders in an organization or a program or by smaller representative groups such as the NAC. Sometimes the nature of the decision or time constraints necessitate that a designated leader or authority decide—and appropriately so. However, given the positive effects of participation on change, those who lead organizations, programs, needs assessment projects, and relevant steering committees should involve stakeholders in decision making as much as feasibly possible. Procedures 18–24 become useful tools for doing so.

Assessing Progress

Is the action plan working well? Are desired processes and anticipated effects taking hold? What new challenges have emerged? Are refinements or adjustments warranted? Assessing progress as the action plan is implemented keeps postassessment on track by documenting successes and exposing problems. Targeted solution strategies well suited to address identified needs may prove fatal if unenthusiastic implementers drag their feet, bad-mouth efforts, or sabotage plans. Even eager implementers may block progress if they lack effective skills for doing the work required (see Chapter 5). Discovering such problems, as well as successes, should focus attention in useful ways. Difficulties, for example, should trigger problem solving, which furthers learning and builds capacity for change. Accomplishments also should prompt celebrations that support momentum and inspire continued action for change.

Essentially Procedures 1–24 in Table 3.1 all may be used (or adapted) to assess progress during postassessment. Some are especially suitable for collecting data (e.g., *Procedure 3: Choosing Corners, Procedure 5: Cooperative Interviews, Procedure 8: Pluses/Wishes, Procedure 9: PMI/PPP, Procedure 11: Graffiti/Carousel*), others for analyzing it (e.g., *Procedure 12: Concept Formation* for qualitative information), and others for making sense of results (e.g., *Procedure 6: Roundtable/Roundrobin, Procedure 14: Force Field Analysis, Procedure 17: Rubric Reflections*).

Consider the following steps for determining which procedures will be most useful for assessing implementation progress in your own needs assessment situation.

- First, determine which aspects of the action plan to evaluate and frame appropriate questions (see Chapter 6, especially Table 6.1).
- Second, determine appropriate data sources such as administrators, staff, clients, or archival documents.
- Third, review directions for facilitating the procedures (Figures 3.1–3.24) and consider which are most useful for obtaining data from identified sources to address the questions.
- Fourth, whenever analyzing qualitative information, consider involving the NAC (or other appropriate groups) by facilitating *Procedure 12: Concept Formation.*
- Fifth, involve appropriate needs assessment committees and/or staff at large in interpreting what the results or findings mean. Although all of the procedures can be adapted to stimulate such conversations, Procedures 10–17 are especially useful because they strategically aim to develop shared understandings (see Table 3.1, Column B).

We recognize that numerous issues relevant to evaluation and assessment should be considered in addition to those noted here. For example, both the validity and the reliability of methods, instruments, samples, data, and analyses warrant serious attention because technical concerns such as these underpin (or undermine) confidence in results. Why bother collecting data on implementation efforts if surveys are flawed, respondents unrepresentative, or analyses inadequate? Most research and evaluation textbooks address these (and other) technical aspects of assessment in detail, all of which merit attention (see Chapter 6 for recommended resources). Here, however, we simply alert those responsible for assessing implementation progress to three final considerations when selecting procedures:

1. *Time.* What are your time constraints? Note the approximate facilitation time required for each procedure as well as required materials. When time for preparation or facilitation is short, consider procedures that are quick and simple and demand few materials. When longer periods of time are available, consider procedures that more fully involve participants in grappling with issues, information, or decisions.

2. *Confidentiality.* Does private versus public participation matter? These procedures should not be used to collect, analyze, or interpret data if social interaction will inappropriately compromise

validity or reliability. However, when conversations can provide credible information or produce adequate analyses and interpretations, consider these procedures to assess implementation progress. When working with large numbers of people, especially focus on those procedures that use small groups to maximize involvement.

3. *Precision.* How precise must data or analyses be for confidence in results? When precision matters, then valid and reliable tests, surveys, interviews, or observations will better serve assessment efforts, as will strict adherence to analysis protocols. However, whenever general patterns, themes, or interpretations can adequately capture the essence of postassessment progress, consider using the procedures in this chapter because they meaningfully involve people (individually and collectively) in conceptualizing, articulating, and formalizing lessons learned, which strengthens commitment to change.

Highlights of the Chapter

Needs assessment essentially is about organizational change. Postassessment involves creating, implementing, and assessing a plan that translates solution strategies into doable actions. This chapter assists needs assessors in facilitating relevant activities.

1. The ultimate goal of postassessment is to use needs assessment information to make appropriate changes.

2. Foundations of change reveal its dimensions (external and internal) and point to factors that matter for success (collaboration, facilitation, mission, knowledge of change, leadership).

3. External, observable dimensions of change occur when people act in new ways, use resources differently, and develop new understandings or beliefs about practice.

4. Internal, hidden dimensions of change occur when people experience discomfort, fear, anxiety, tension, confusion, or a sense of loss from doing things differently.

5. Making personal and collective meaning of change increases commitment to implementation.

6. A double dozen facilitation procedures (see Table 3.1) strategically accomplish four broad purposes: (a) promoting positive interpersonal relations, (b) developing shared understandings, (c) prioritizing and finalizing decisions, and (d) assessing progress. These procedures and purposes enable needs assessors to successfully carry out the steps of postassessment (see Table 1.3).

4

Positive Approaches to Conflict

Weathering Interpersonal Storms

A system cannot change without experiencing conflict. How it is handled profoundly determines the success of the effort to change. Furthermore, there is a strong similarity between the process involved in successful change efforts and that involved in constructive conflict resolution.

—Marcus, 2006, p. 445

❖ INTRODUCTION

Striving to conduct the perfect needs assessment may be a noble goal, but in the real world, such a process doesn't exist. Wise needs assessors will prepare to respond to the unexpected, especially during postassessment when change will surely make waves. No matter how thoughtful or well executed the needs assessment, its action-planning process, or implementation activities, somewhere along the way something inevitably goes wrong. Sometimes organizational structures unexpectedly shift, or individual attitudes or aptitudes block progress (see Chapter 5). In many instances, however, change creates conditions ripe for interpersonal (or intergroup) conflict. For example, administrators enacting new policies disrupt familiar or comfortable staff routines, service providers eager to implement solution strategies collide with less enthusiastic coworkers dragging their feet, or departments clash when reallocated resources threaten to eliminate cherished programs.

For many years social psychologists have studied conflict in settings and cultures around the world. Drawing from that discipline, we begin by defining conflict and situating it within needs assessment contexts. We then briefly present two theoretical frameworks that underpin positive approaches to resolving conflict: *conflict strategies theory* (D. W. Johnson & F. P. Johnson, 2009) and *constructive conflict resolution theory* (Deutsch, 1973). These theories reveal two sets of skills useful for managing conflict constructively. The first involves structuring cooperative goals among those carrying out postassessment tasks. The second involves negotiating for mutual problem solving when conflict occurs. Derived from these theories and skills, we present five competencies that needs assessors and organizational leaders can master to proactively and productively weather the interpersonal storms that inevitably will surface as postassessment unfolds.

❖ RECOGNIZING CONFLICT IN POSTASSESSMENT

Deutsch (1973, p. 10) defines conflict succinctly: "A *conflict* exists whenever *incompatible* activities occur." Incompatible activities are those that block, delay, or prevent the accomplishment of goals. In postassessment, such activities impede implementation of the needs assessment action plan. Consider the following scenarios:

- A key leader who is the driving force behind the needs assessment effort gets a new job and leaves the organization; the director of the organization now assigns others to spearhead the process, whether or not they are equipped to take on this responsibility.
- Members of a minority community who are essential to the change feel uncomfortable coming to the school building where meetings are held, so they largely don't participate in implementation planning sessions; this dismays those coordinating the sessions and puts the quality of the solution strategies at risk.

- A county manager whose support will be necessary to implement any change in the organization comes late to meetings and talks loudly to anyone who will listen about what a waste of time they are; this angers those who are working overtime to make change successful.
- Line staff who feel overwhelmed with what is already on their professional plates do not respond to phone or electronic messages from the needs assessment committee (NAC) because they fear more tasks will be added to already heavy workloads; this obstructs progress and annoys committee members.

Conflicts like these are part and parcel of change efforts and can fluctuate over time. For example, people who are enthusiastic at one point may lose interest when they see the implementation evolving in ways that differ from their vision or if the timeline stretches too far into the future. Others may get fired up as the implementation unfolds by prospects of better meeting clients' needs.

Regardless of the issue or who is involved, every conflict holds the potential to disrupt, derail, or abruptly halt change. Whether that happens depends on how disputants manage the conflict. For example, fear, anger, and frustration can trigger defensive responses that lead to win-lose outcomes, destructive actions, and long-term bitterness. By contrast, working to understand diverse perspectives, appreciate underlying interests, and develop mutually favorable solutions can lead to win-win outcomes that enhance efforts and support positive relationships.

Needs assessors who choose a constructive path for managing conflict do so with intention. They create a climate conducive to positive conflict by structuring cooperative relations whenever people meet to work on postassessment tasks. They observe the interpersonal dynamics that unfold and recognize, name, and confront conflicts that occur. They understand alternative responses to conflict and the likely effects of each. They apply and model integrative negotiation skills to mutually resolve problems. They also assist coworkers and clients to use these skills so that everyone can benefit.

❖ THEORETICAL FRAMEWORKS FOR CONSTRUCTIVE CONFLICT RESOLUTION

Two theories from social psychology, each well grounded in empirical research (see Deutsch, 1973, 2006; D. W. Johnson & F. P. Johnson, 2009;

Pruitt & Carnevale, 1993), provide insights into the dynamics of conflict. Both theories underscore the importance of relationships in determining the course of interpersonal conflict and especially how that course either supports or impedes change efforts during postassessment.

Conflict Strategies Theory

When conflict occurs, how do those involved respond? Do they push to get their way? Seek to sidestep the issues? Appease people in the interest of harmony? Strike a deal to get part of what they want? Problem solve collectively to satisfy everyone? Conflict strategies theory (D. W. Johnson & F. P. Johnson, 2009) outlines these five responses (see Figure 4.1). Basically, people face two types of concerns in conflict situations: (a) achieving desired goals/interests and

Figure 4.1   Conflict Strategies Theory (see D. W. Johnson & F. P. Johnson, 2009)

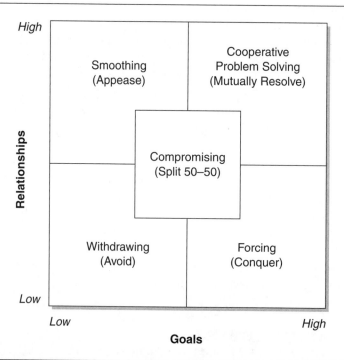

Source: Adapted from Johnson & Johnson (2005b, p. 4:2). Copyright 1975 by David W. Johnson. Reprinted with permission.

(b) maintaining positive working relationships. Placing these dual concerns on intersecting continua from *low* to *high* importance suggests five strategies for addressing conflict:

- *Forcing* means achieving one's own goals at the expense of others'. Relationships don't matter; self-interests do. Like opponents struggling against each other during a chess match, one person's winning requires another's defeat. Someone loses, and relationships often suffer. A state department head, for example, who suddenly mandates a new procedure, regardless of its likely effect on staff and clients, may nominally implement a change but create organizational dysfunction as angry people focus their energy on circumventing the new requirement.

- *Withdrawing* means giving up one's personal goals and positive relationships with others. It is a natural response to forcing. The person's actions say, literally, "I'm out of here." Neither self-interest in the goal nor relationships matter. Hiding or running away to avoid conflict resolves nothing, making everyone a loser. A team member, for example, who repeatedly misses meetings and refuses to respond to voice mail, text messages, or e-mail simultaneously blocks the implementation process and creates distrust.

- *Smoothing* means giving up one's personal goals to maintain positive relationships with others at the highest level possible. Appeasing may satisfy others, but it requires sacrificing self-interests. In an assessment context, a steering committee member may smile and willingly agree with the implementation plan but not express misgivings or desired alternatives, concerned about the tension or discomfort that expressing these may cause others.

- *Compromising* means using give-and-take to create a 50-50 split when someone's personal goals and relationships with others are both moderately important. Seeing the benefits of partial gain, people decide to settle for something, which seems better than getting nothing. In a large-scale change effort, for example, a participant may agree to include different items on an agency's intake form in exchange for new data entry procedures.

- *Problem solving* means cooperative negotiation aimed at maximizing joint outcomes. Both self-interests and relationships with others matter. When people consider everyone's interests, they can create integrative solutions so that everyone benefits. Such win-win results maximize joint outcomes. For example, when needs assessment data documented that a food bank was turning away neighborhood residents while serving people from other zip codes, integrative negotiation led to a new system that guaranteed local clients access and others either access or assistance in reaching nearby sources of free food.

Conflict is fraught with complexity, but conflict strategies theory, the dual concerns model, provides a helpful lens through which to assess it. When people force their way during a conflict ("My way or the highway") or when they withdraw to avoid the situation ("I won't talk about it"), little hope exists for constructive outcomes. In the context of postassessment activities, progress surely will suffer, if not come to a grinding halt.

The prudent needs assessor recognizes that competence in successfully navigating conflict requires skill in using all five strategies. At times it may be in one's best interest to stand firm (force) when principles or values matter deeply or to exit gracefully (withdraw) from unworkable situations. Doing so, however, may jeopardize future relationships with colleagues. If people hope to work with others over time or in future endeavors, finding ways to mutually problem solve usually produces the most constructive outcomes and positive working relationships. Next, we consider how integrative problem solving is enhanced when people perceive their interdependence in achieving meaningful cooperative goals.

Constructive Conflict Resolution Theory

Deutsch's (1973, 2006) constructive conflict resolution theory is a second framework for thinking about interpersonal conflict. It illuminates the dynamics of conflict by identifying the different goal structures that exist among individuals and how those structures influence behaviors in conflict situations (see Figure 4.2). Originating from social interdependence theory (Deutsch, 1949a, 1949b, 2006; D. W. Johnson & F. P. Johnson, 2009; D. W. Johnson & R. T. Johnson, 1989, 2005a, 2009), research suggests that cooperative goals make individuals positively interdependent, creating situations in which people need each other to succeed. By contrast, competitive goals make individuals negatively interdependent, leading to situations in which people can succeed or win only when others fail or lose. Constructive conflict resolution

Figure 4.2   Constructive Conflict Resolution Theory (see Deutsch, 1973)

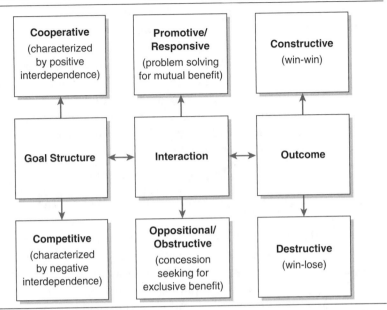

Source: From Stevahn, L., & King, J. A. (2005). Managing conflict constructively in program evaluation. *Evaluation, 11*(4), 415–427.

theory indicates that the goal structure that exists among individuals or groups in conflict situations (cooperative or competitive) influences interpersonal or intergroup interactions (promotive/responsive or oppositional/obstructive), which determines the resolution of the conflict (constructive or destructive).

Simply put, individuals' responses to conflict tend to differ according to their degree of investment in each other's success. Mutual problem solving (similar to cooperative problem solving in the dual concerns model) likely occurs when people perceive that each person's individual success depends on the success of the entire group, and vice versa. In needs assessment, for example, when members of a data analysis team perceive that they truly need the unique perspectives and skills of all team members to complete the job, such as when the skills of both quantitative and qualitative experts are required, the more it makes sense to engage in problem solving behavior when conflicts arise. Relationships matter, and cooperative goal structures that require interdependent efforts tend to develop caring relationships, even if only instrumental, that lead to constructive interactions and outcomes.

Experimental and correlational research over many years indicates that cooperative versus competitive goal structures result in friendlier, more trusting attitudes among individuals; increased sensitivity to common interests; more open and honest communication of relevant information; and greater responsiveness to each other's needs (Deutsch, 1973, 2006). Knowing how goal structures affect human interaction enables needs assessors to better analyze situational contexts of assessment by noticing cooperative and competitive activities and intentionally structuring positive interdependence into postassessment tasks carried out by various committees. In competitive contexts participatory interactions are likely to fail if individuals compete to meet their personal needs at others' expense.

❖ SKILLS FOR CONSTRUCTIVE CONFLICT RESOLUTION

Theories and conceptual frameworks are helpful for decision making in conflict situations, but successful action requires skills. Two critical sets of skills include (a) structuring goals and tasks cooperatively and (b) using integrative negotiation procedures. Mastering these skills requires training, practice, and reflection. Here we outline key practical components.

Structuring Cooperative Goals

Cooperative contexts set the stage for managing conflict constructively. One of the most important skills for accomplishing this is how to structure positive interdependence into social situations and needs assessment tasks. Doing so builds the capacity for productive working relationships which, in turn, leads to problem solving rather than less productive responses to conflict. Although the frequency of interaction among participants during postassessment varies (potentially more continuous for those who are actively involved in the implementation), each interaction provides an opportunity for examining existing goal structures and establishing conditions that support cooperative goals and relationships.

Interactive approaches allow needs assessors to structure cooperative goals and meaningful involvement in the assessment, which generally increases people's commitment to proposed changes (see Chapter 3). Promoting cooperative relationships begins by using positive interdependence as a tool for structuring tasks in ways that require collaborative interaction for success. Positive interdependence can be structured into almost any group task, including those that comprise the steps of postassessment (see Table 1.3). Whether finalizing solution strategies, creating the action plan, monitoring implementation, or evaluating the entire needs assessment, arrange tasks in ways such that everyone's contributions will be interconnected and perceived as necessary for success. Start by establishing and emphasizing the common goal; then arrange materials, roles, and incentives in ways that foster coordinated efforts. For example, designate separate yet interconnected roles/jobs, supply shared sets of materials/resources, and provide team rewards/celebrations for successful accomplishment of mutual goals. Arrangements like these highlight the mutual interdependence that exists among participants and provide incentives for teamwork.

Many of the double dozen procedures in Chapter 3 demonstrate how to structure positive interdependence into postassessment tasks (see Table 3.1). By consistently using such procedures, needs assessors help establish the types of cooperative relationships conducive to resolving conflicts constructively when they occur. The following examples illustrate how various procedures use positive interdependence to strengthen cooperative interaction.

1. The chair of the NAC wishes to facilitate discussion on how best to build commitment and support throughout the organization for implementing the postassessment action plan. To ensure that all voices are part of the discussion, the chair facilitates *Procedure 5: Cooperative Interviews.* After forming groups of three, the chair explains that each participant will take a turn enacting each role—*interviewer, responder,* or *recorder*—to address the following questions: "What is a change that you have made in your professional practice—something effective that you routinely do now that you did not when you first began? What influenced you to make the change? What did you notice, and how did you feel as you first engaged in the early stages of making the change? What was it like trying something new? What factors contributed to your ultimate success?" Rotating the interconnected roles after each round and recording each person's input on a single, shared answer sheet highlights the mutual interdependence necessary to complete the group task. So, too, does asking each team to look over all recorded input to compare and contrast characteristics across stories, especially noting similar themes that emerge as well as unique outlier factors. Such focused conversations enable participants to build positive relationships through respectful listening and understand more

clearly underlying assumptions of what makes change successful. These assumptions can then be used to propose concrete strategies for implementing the action plan in ways that will build support, commitment, and success.

2. A team of needs assessors has obtained observations from numerous stakeholders—service providers as well as recipients—to monitor implementation of the postassessment action plan. Knowing that involvement will likely fuel further commitment to implementing the plan, the needs assessors decide to review the summarized observations by facilitating *Procedure 10: Jigsaw*. All departments send a representative to the review meeting, and clients from diverse ethnic communities also are invited to participate. The needs assessors arrange participants in heterogeneous groups of four (mixed by role, job, department, programs, services provided/received, etc.). Then, like a jigsaw puzzle, each person in each group receives a different summary sheet. The first sheet contains client observations; the second, observations from those who develop and deliver programs; the third, observations from middle management; the fourth, observations from support staff. The goal is for everyone in the small group to construct a comprehensive picture of how implementation is progressing by using information from all four summary sheets. To accomplish this, participants read their unique information and present key points to other members of their group. Prior to presenting, facilitators ask all participants to find someone from a different group whose summary sheet matches their own (e.g., two individuals responsible for client observations pair up). These expert pairs review their information and discuss effective ways to present main points once back in their original groups of four. After each of the four presentations, facilitators then ask all groups to determine how well the implementation is progressing and suggest actions to further enhance efforts. Positive interdependence promotes strong connections among participants as each clearly sees how his or her piece of the puzzle is needed to complete the whole. In addition, everyone gains comprehensive knowledge about progress on implementing the action plan.

3. A needs assessor who requires input or reactions from a large group can facilitate *Procedure 11: Graffiti/Carousel* to collect information efficiently while creating positive interdependence.

Sheets of flipchart paper, each labeled with a different topic or category (e.g., infrastructure that will support a particular solution strategy, likely challenges that service providers will face if the strategy becomes part of the action plan, resources helpful to enacting the strategy, inconveniences that the strategy may create, anticipated benefits of the strategy, other strategies that may address the identified need), either can be rotated around tables until each group has had an opportunity to write on each sheet or can be taped to the wall allowing people to write on the sheets during a wall walk. Subsequently, *Procedure 12: Concept Formation* is used to involve each group in analyzing what has been written or posted on one of the flipchart sheets and then report major themes/outcomes to the entire gathering. The common goal of collectively understanding everyone's ideas highlights the positive interdependence among participants and the imperative of everyone contributing to get the job done.

Negotiating for Mutual Gain

Needs assessors can use negotiation to resolve conflicts that occur during postassessment. Essentially, negotiation involves individuals (or groups) in an interactive process that can be underpinned by competitive or cooperative relations. As described previously, different goal orientations affect interactions and outcomes. In particular, competitive situations fuel distributive negotiation in which disputants try to maximize personal outcomes at the expense of others. Such negotiation entails win-lose battles as each side tries to defeat the other by coercing concessions (similar to forcing in the dual concerns model). Numerous strategies and tactics for negotiating competitively exist and have been widely published (see D. W. Johnson & F. P. Johnson, 2009; Lewicki, Saunders, & Barry, 2010; Pruitt & Carnevale, 1993).

By contrast, cooperative situations fuel integrative negotiation in which people seek to maximize everyone's outcomes. This type of negotiation involves disputants in mutual problem solving for joint benefits (like cooperative problem solving in the dual concerns model). Skills for negotiating cooperatively include the following (see Brett, 2007; Fisher, Ury, & Patton, 1991; Johnson, 1967; D. W. Johnson & F. P. Johnson, 2009; Johnson & Johnson, 2005b; Lewicki Saunders & Barry, 2010; Stevahn & King, 2005):

- Expressing cooperative intentions
- Mutually defining the conflict

- Stating wants
- Expressing feelings
- Explaining underlying reasons/interests
- Reversing perspectives to communicate understanding
- Generating multiple integrative solutions that attend to all interests
- Reaching agreement on a mutual solution
- Processing the effectiveness of the problem-solving process

The importance of developing expertise in integrative negotiation, along with other relevant interpersonal skills such as communication, group facilitation, group processing, teamwork/collaboration, and intercultural competence (see Stevahn, King, Ghere, & Minnema, 2005), becomes clear when you realize the extent of interaction required among people throughout a change effort. Conflicts will occur and resolutions will be determined one way or another—constructively or destructively. By mastering and using integrative negotiation skills, needs assessors can better influence constructive outcomes. Figure 4.3 provides an example of what this might sound like in practice.

Figure 4.3   Integrative Negotiation

Steps	Needs Assessor	Service Provider
1. <u>Confront the conflict and express cooperative intentions.</u>	I'd like to talk with you about a concern I have with the new documentation procedure specified in the needs assessment action plan. It doesn't seem to be working well. I care about figuring out how to make this tracking system doable for all of us.	Yes, let's talk. I also have some serious concerns about the new tracking system. The documentation process has placed quite a burden on me.
2. <u>State what you want.</u>	I want the client interview forms completed in a timely manner.	I want to use my time to provide services to our clients, not do paperwork.

Steps	Needs Assessor	Service Provider
3. <u>Express how you feel</u>.	I feel frustrated that I'm supposed to track client progress, but don't get all of the information I need. I care about doing my job well and about the success of the action plan.	I feel angry when I already carry a full workload and then face new tasks that demand additional time but don't seem to provide much "value added."
4. <u>Explain your reasons</u>.	The organization relies on the client interviews to document progress for program funding. The director holds me personally accountable for weekly reports that summarize how programs are addressing client needs. I can't prepare those reports without complete sets of information. The interviews also can help our organization personalize client services.	Doing my job well means serving the personal needs of my clients. I put in long hours every day doing just that. I am totally dedicated to those I serve, and spending additional time on paperwork doesn't help them or me.
5. <u>Reverse perspectives</u> by communicating your understanding of the other person's wants, feelings, and reasons.	I understand that you feel overwhelmed with your workload and irritated when asked to do "one more thing" that doesn't seem necessary. Your first priority is devoting time to your clients and serving them well, not spending time on extra paperwork. You learn the details of their personal needs as you interact with them every day.	My understanding of your situation is that you're feeling pressure each week from the director; your integrity is on the line when it comes to providing those reports. The documentation matters to the organization because it's linked to program funding. You need the interview forms completed on time to be able to do your job, which you want to do well.

(Continued)

Figure 4.3 (Continued)

Steps	Needs Assessor	Service Provider
6. Generate solutions that benefit everyone.	A. We could streamline interview forms to make them less time consuming. B. We could ask clients to complete the forms prior to arriving for services.	C. We could tape interviews and then have clerical staff transcribe them and complete the paperwork. D. We could incorporate focus group interviews into service sessions.
7. Mutually agree on one solution.	I like the focus group idea best. We could conduct sessions together and take turns facilitating discussions and documenting input.	Sounds good. Clients will benefit from the interaction, I will learn more about their needs, and you will get timely input for your report. Let's try it.

❖ CONFLICT COMPETENCIES FOR NEEDS ASSESSORS

Understanding conflict theories and developing conflict competencies equip needs assessors with tools to increase effectiveness. First, with an eye for conflict, they can better analyze the social context of organizations or programs contemplating or conducting needs assessment initiatives. Second, they can better identify people's responses to conflict and devise appropriate ways to deal with those behaviors. Third, when conflict occurs they can facilitate and participate in resolving it constructively. Fourth, they can establish project, program, or organizational norms for managing conflict by structuring tasks that promote cooperative relationships. Fifth, they can better reflect on their own reactions and responses in conflict situations. We elaborate each of these applications below.

Analyze the Social Context

Equipped with conceptual understanding of conflict and skills for managing it constructively, needs assessors can effectively analyze the conflict landscape of an organization or program. Just as analyzing the political context helps one decide if it will be feasible to conduct a needs assessment, examining the nature, frequency, and patterns of cooperation and conflict within the organization or program also reveals valuable information. Both external facilitators (who serve as outside sources to organizations/programs) and internal facilitators (who work full-time in an organization/program) can benefit from habitually asking questions about (a) existing goal structures within organizations/programs, (b) the breadth and depth of cooperative interaction among individuals in such contexts, and (c) how those individuals respond to conflict. Helpful questions to guide analyses follow.

Goal Structures

What types of goal structures predominantly exist within the organization or program? When and where do people work cooperatively, competitively, or individualistically? To what extent does the organization/program value cooperative efforts and mutual problem solving? How does the organization/program support or reward such efforts? What are the mutual goals to which everyone is committed? To what extent is mutual problem solving a way of life? What rules, routines, and norms support cooperative interaction and constructive conflict resolution?

Cooperative Interaction

What tasks within the organization/program require people to coordinate their ideas, resources, and energy to be successful? Do cooperative tasks have well-defined mutual goals? Are teams rewarded for success? What types of incentives make individuals want to work together? How do individuals benefit from working together? What motivates cooperative behavior within the program/ organization? What types of tangible rewards exist for collaborative work? How do people coordinate their efforts? Does the physical work space and arrangement of desks/furniture promote or block cooperative interaction?

Conflict Situations

What types of conflicts occur in the program/organization? How do people respond? Do they predominantly force, withdraw, smooth, compromise, or problem solve? What communication patterns unfold in conflict situations? To what extent do people hold positive attitudes toward resolving conflict? Do individuals express cooperative intentions for mutual problem solving when conflicts occur? Do leaders model and use constructive conflict procedures?

Recognize Conflict Behaviors

Change efforts can create conflict for individuals, even when they are willing participants in postassessment activities. Meetings can become a stage on which individuals enact their personal responses to action planning and proposed changes, and problems can also arise apart from meetings, as people chat in the lunchroom, circulate e-mail or text messages, or hold TGIF (Thank Goodness It's Friday) discussions after hours. In the world of practice, individuals can work actively to deflect, slow, or sabotage change, perhaps especially in large, multisite organizations where, at best, communication is challenging given geographic and/or social distance.

The five conflict strategies in the dual concerns model (see Figure 4.1) can be used to analyze conflicts that surface during postassessment. Awareness of these approaches to conflict helps needs assessors, along with others leading the implementation, devise appropriate responses, remembering that any of the five may be best depending on circumstances. Because one of the approaches, cooperative problem solving, facilitates positive interaction, it is typically the most constructive for dealing with interpersonal issues. It is also most often the approach pursued by individuals who want to engage each other in ways that clarify alternative perspectives to create win-win solutions. Consider, however, the other four approaches: forcing, withdrawing, smoothing, or compromising. Needs assessors may see the following baker's dozen of individual responses divided among them.

Forcing

The act of forcing focuses on accomplishing a personal goal at the risk of alienating people and destroying long-term relations. Six examples of forcing include:

1. The strong individual who dominates group interactions, including people with positional power (the boss, the team leader) and people with domineering personalities and powerful interpersonal styles.

2. The person who generates and thrives on conflict, the naysayer, she who doesn't want to negotiate, he who opposes the action item (doesn't want resources to go to that), and that unhappy individual (such as "Debbie Downer" on *Saturday Night Live*) who lives with a negative attitude.

3. The person who never comes to meetings on time and disrupts what is going on by arriving loudly (as if to say, "Look at me!") well after the announced start time.

4. The person who hates any type of warm-up activity perceived as too "touchy-feely" and asks openly, "When do we link arms and sing 'Kumbaya'?"

5. The person who needs to feel important in the group and always explains the multiple activities going on in his or her world ("Behold me busy!").

6. The person who attends meetings sporadically or misses meetings in a random pattern so that he or she never knows what is going on and has to be updated by those who do attend.

Recognizing when people are seeking personal goals (getting their way, feeling important or in control, or dodging the change process) allows needs assessors to refocus efforts on the broader goals of the implementation and on relationships with others. In some cases this requires meeting force with force by having someone in authority articulate norms and hold people accountable for altering their behavior. Sometimes it means labeling their behavior so they can see its consequences and choose to change. At other times it means ignoring the behavior. The key is to examine both the goals of the larger action plan and the long-term interpersonal relationships required to make a successful change and then respond accordingly. Truly, such interventions may be more art than science.

Withdrawing

If people withdraw from the implementation process, it is difficult to move forward. Three forms of withdrawing include the following:

1. The person who intentionally misses every meeting, despite a requirement or expectation to attend

2. The person whose body shows up but who doesn't pay attention, choosing instead to talk, text, pound on a computer, knit, read a magazine, or do something else unrelated to the discussion

3. The quiet person who doesn't readily participate out loud in the meeting, perhaps because of a style preference, a personality trait, a cultural norm, or discomfort in that situation

Withdrawing neither achieves the goal in question nor builds relationships. You can address the first two forms (those who don't show up or who do and don't participate) by letting individuals know the effects of their actions, expecting change, and encouraging compliance. People in the third category (the quiet types) present a different challenge. If they are shy or if their culture rewards silence and quiet attendance, they may appear to be withdrawing when in fact they are mentally focused and engaged yet outwardly behaving in ways ingrained or comfortable. The needs assessor in that case must first recognize this and then structure activities that allow everyone opportunities to participate without threatening individuals for whom meaningful involvement doesn't involve speaking publicly. The interactive procedures in Chapter 3 illustrate structures that invite meaningful and comfortable involvement from everyone.

Smoothing

Every organization needs people who build relationships and make others feel good about ongoing activities. They are the people who regularly bring snacks, acknowledge birthdays, and provide support during times of personal crises. When smoothing takes precedence over achieving an action plan's goals, however, implementation has a problem. Two types of smoothers can derail a change process:

1. The person who, having survived multiple change efforts ("This, too, shall pass"), supports the status quo, firmly believing that "it ain't broken," so why ruffle feathers of coworkers who are friends

2. The person who avoids meaningful interaction like the plague by giggling, making jokes that detract from the issue at hand, chatting during meetings, or agreeing with anything simply to agree, thinking that this is what it takes to gain approval from others

Again, when you observe these behaviors, you can label them and let people see the likely effects of their actions and either encourage or require them to get with the program. Another possibility is to work with such individuals to revise or shape the action plan in ways that are more personally relevant—that is, to help them better understand and buy into the implementation goals.

Compromising

In situations where cooperative negotiation is impossible for whatever reasons, compromise may be the most positive option available to needs assessors. It is important to remember that, unlike the other response categories, the compromiser is at least partly willing to work toward the stated goals and to maintain relationships. Nevertheless, two kinds of compromisers may prove problematic:

1. The compromiser with a tit-for-tat mentality ("I'll let you have this but only if you give in on the points that are important to me")

2. The person who sincerely asks, "What's in it for me?" and will engage in the process only if he or she perceives an outcome of personal value

Two previous suggestions for dealing with smoothers apply here as well: Label the behavior and expect change, or engage with the individual to create a personal connection to the action plan. Building positive commitment may foster increased ownership of the change process. Because these problematic responses seem to hold a competitive edge, it also may be helpful to remind such individuals that this is not a give-or-take contest.

These 13 responses to change (and variations thereof) point to the continuing challenges that needs assessors face in postassessment. Individuals may force during a meeting and then withdraw afterward if they don't get their way. Inveterate smoothers may find it impossible to move beyond muffins and warm fuzzies, knowing the harsh reality of meaningful transformation. Veteran employees who have watched innovations come and go will need some reason to believe that implementing the action plan is really going to enhance their lives and improve the organization. Needs assessors, as well as others in charge of implementation, can support the change process by structuring activities to build cooperative interdependence and create accountability for individual roles throughout postassessment. They also can teach and use integrative negotiation for mutual problem solving to manage conflicts in ways that constructively advance change.

Facilitate Mutual Problem Solving

Numerous factors affect conflict situations. One is the nature of the issues themselves (see Deutsch, 1973). Those that tap into deeply ingrained values (e.g., ideals, principles, ideologies) and beliefs (e.g., religious, philosophical, moral) are more challenging to resolve than those that deal with control over resources (e.g., money, space, time) or preferences (e.g., dim lights in the office, culturally appropriate snacks at meetings, relaxed dress codes on Fridays). Other factors include power relations (low vs. high), people's abilities to manage anger and control emotions, levels of trust and suspicion, cultural differences/considerations, and intergroup conflicts (involving multiple parties or coalitions) versus interpersonal conflicts (concerning two or only a few individuals).

Regardless of these factors, needs assessors systematically can guide interactions toward mutual problem solving and integrative solutions in postassessment. This can take the form of actually using constructive skills when personally facing conflicts, mediating the conflicts of others, or teaching the skills to others when appropriate, as it often is within an organization, a program, or a community. Although needs assessment itself is an unlikely tool to address organizational conflict directly, the actions of people throughout can contribute to influencing the various pathways that conflict may take, whether constructive or destructive.

Create Cooperative Norms

Needs assessors can help create organizational, program, or project norms for constructive conflict resolution by structuring cooperative interaction among participants. Pragmatically this entails repeatedly incorporating positive interdependence into postassessment tasks. The cooperative relationships likely to develop not only promote stakeholder commitment to the needs assessment; they also help build organizational infrastructure that grounds and supports problem-solving negotiation when conflicts occur.

Know Thyself

Understanding conflict theories enables needs assessors to better reflect on their own reactions and responses to conflict. We all have different triggers, tolerances, and thresholds in conflict situations. Thinking about personal response patterns in relation to conflict strategies theory, for example, may help individuals become more strategic in responding. It pays to pick and choose battles, as well as how to engage in them. Needs assessors can systematically choose when to problem solve, compromise, smooth, withdraw, or force by weighing dual concerns to determine the importance of each (attaining goals and maintaining positive working relationships). Better understanding these possibilities paves the way for dealing with conflicts intentionally rather than haphazardly.

❖ REALISTIC EXPECTATIONS

The English language contains multiple terms for conflict: *dispute, dissension, disagreement, controversy, strife, friction, dissonance, argument, discord,* and so on (Stevahn & King, 2005). These words speak of its common occurrence in human experience. People who are unable or who refuse to engage in dialogue, casting their competing values only in shades of black and white, will never find mutual solutions. Although conflicts typically are complex, the theories presented in this chapter, along with skills that promote positive outcomes, are supported by an abundance of empirical evidence. Conflicts are inevitable in needs assessment, perhaps especially in postassessment aimed at implementing change, but we understand it now in ways that were not thought of 100 years ago.

What, then, are realistic expectations for needs assessors in conflict situations? We believe they can (a) recognize and expect that conflicts will occur, (b) assess organization and program contexts to determine the extent to which cooperative relationships exist among individuals and where cooperative goal structures are needed, (c) observe how individuals respond to conflict, (d) use appropriate conflict strategies and negotiation skills to keep postassessment implementations on track, (e) constantly reflect on personal approaches to conflict, and (f) practice the skills that comprise constructive conflict resolution. Throughout, remember that social context is crucial. Attempting to use integrative negotiation in a competitive context will be frustrating at best and, based on consistent research evidence, likely doomed to fail. Basically, success in managing conflict will be possible only when needs assessors and leaders work to change organizational structures from competitive/individualistic to cooperative. The role of the needs assessor is to recognize the impact of social structures and relationships and work to make them cooperative. Doing so supports positive change even in challenging postassessment situations.

Highlights of the Chapter

Conflict is inevitable in needs assessment, perhaps even more so in postassessment as people create and implement an action plan. This chapter presents theories, frameworks, and skills that needs assessors can use to manage conflict constructively.

1. Conflict occurs when incompatible activities block, delay, or prevent the accomplishment of goals.

2. Conflict can be resolved constructively through integrative (win-win) negotiation or destructively through distributive (win-lose) negotiation.

3. Conflict strategies theory (D. W. Johnson & F. P. Johnson, 2009) highlights dual concerns that people face in conflict (achieving goals and maintaining positive relationships) from which five responses emerge: forcing, withdrawing, smoothing, compromising, and problem solving.

4. Constructive conflict resolution theory (Deutsch, 1973, 2006) indicates that goal structures (cooperative or competitive) influence interactions (promotive/responsive or oppositional/obstructive), which, in turn, determine outcomes (constructive or destructive).

5. Needs assessors can structure cooperative goals in postassessment activities by building positive interdependence into tasks (emphasizing the common goal, assigning unique yet interconnected roles, arranging shared/jigsawed resources, providing joint rewards/recognition for success).

6. Needs assessors should use integrative negotiation skills, including expressing cooperative intentions, mutually defining the conflict, stating wants, expressing feelings, explaining reasons/interests, communicating understanding of alternative perspectives, generating mutually beneficial solutions, reaching agreement on which solution to pursue, and processing the effectiveness of problem solving efforts.

7. Needs assessors proactively promote success by (a) analyzing the needs assessment context for structures that influence social relations, (b) recognizing conflict behaviors, (c) facilitating mutual problem solving, (d) creating cooperative norms, and (e) knowing personal reactions and responses in conflict situations.

8. Although numerous factors affect the course of conflict, needs assessors and organizational leaders can realistically influence constructive outcomes by mastering and applying theories and skills that promote cooperative foundations for mutual problem solving.

5

Individual and Organizational Roadblocks

Responding to Unexpected Challenges

Get ready to handle the inevitable obstacles. They always occur. So expect them, anticipate them, and be prepared mentally to deal with them.

—Belasco, 1990, p. 31

❖ INTRODUCTION

Phase III of needs assessment, in which you prioritize solution strategies, create and implement an action plan, and monitor progress, requires that people attend numerous meetings and interact frequently. Think about change efforts you have been part of and recall how different people responded. Some were enthusiastic about everything; others about nothing. Some complained about a heavy workload; others simply buckled down and did the work. Some had the skills necessary to get the job done; others were ill equipped. These types of reactions are common in any organization.

Here we present a framework for thinking about individual characteristics (attitudes and aptitudes) that can block the change process and how needs assessors can respond to facilitate implementation, including a range of logistical factors that support individuals as they move in new directions. We also consider the big picture of implementing an action plan by looking at organizational issues that impede progress and how needs assessors can realistically put structures and support systems in place to orchestrate success, especially when unexpected challenges arise.

❖ INDIVIDUAL CHARACTERISTICS THAT CHALLENGE CHANGE

Every organization has individuals with unique attitudes and aptitudes that require different kinds of responses throughout the change process. Think about people's attitudes (willing or not) and their aptitudes (skills/abilities or lack thereof) to complete the work. When crossed, these two variables result in four potential outcomes (see Table 5.1).

Table 5.1   Individual Attitude/Aptitude Matrix

Aptitude / Attitude		Able to do the work?	
		Yes	*No*
Willing to do the work?	*Yes*	1. Willing and able	2. Willing but unable
	No	3. Unwilling but able	4. Unwilling and unable

Source: © 2004 Jean A. King.

1. *The willing and able.* The first category encompasses those who have both the will and the skills to participate fully in implementation activities. This is the group instrumental in making the action plan a reality. Even so, the potential exists for problems, such as those who "never say never" and end up saddled with too much work. These intrepid contributors want to do everything, perhaps for control, by default, or due to martyrlike personalities. Ever the good citizens, they leap into the

organizational vacuum that the change process creates. Yet, this can be problematic if others become jealous when doers receive perks for engaging in change activities (such as release time, travel to conferences, or extra resources) or keep their distance for fear extra tasks may be added to workloads. An educator once captured this tension by labeling those who constantly took on tasks for change as "élite lepers." Some thought the doers received too many privileges; others avoided them like the plague.

2. *The willing but unable.* In postassessment, leaders of change must attend to those who, for whatever reason, are not able to contribute productively. Not acknowledging this fact puts an unfair burden on those in the organization who can do the job. There are at least two kinds of individuals in this category: people who are unable to do the work (truly underqualified, incompetent, or dead wood drawing a paycheck) and people who are on leave (officially or not) owing to illness or other personal issues. Enthusiastic incompetence is perhaps the scariest of all. Inappropriate, infeasible, or unworkable plans or actions may substantially block overall progress.

3. *The unwilling but able.* There are potentially three types of individuals here, the first being those with inappropriate attitudes. These are the obstructionists, saboteurs, and rumor mongers who purposefully work to destroy the change process. Also included is any leader who elects to delegate implementation/change tasks but chooses not to play an active role. This stymies change through omission rather than commission. The second type consists of well-intended people who hold conflicting values or who don't buy in to the proposed vision, actively fighting it because they think it is a bad idea. The third type is capable individuals who appear willing and assume tasks but never complete them. They say, "Yes, yes," but don't deliver on promises. Like passive or passive-aggressive behavior, not following through on postassessment tasks can easily knock change off course over time if progress is not tracked carefully.

4. *The unwilling and unable.* Talk about a double threat. These are the purposeful naysayers who couple a bad attitude with a lack of skills. In an ideal world, they would lose their jobs rather than poison the change effort or mess it up through their inability to perform.

The point is this. An array of attitudes and aptitudes exists within any organization. Some may block successful implementation because the action plan asks individuals to do things differently. People respond in multiple ways to mandates and requests that alter routines, whether such directives entail small or dramatic change. There may (or may not) be conscious motivation for behaviors that detract from postassessment purposes. Individuals sometimes don't recognize their own negative attitudes or incompetent behaviors, and even though it isn't necessarily intended, such posture prevents progress. The more intentional the "can't," "won't," and "don't do it" behaviors, the more challenging the job of needs assessors.

❖ RESPONDING TO INDIVIDUAL CHALLENGES

Fortunately, there are ways to address individual attitudes and aptitudes that hinder change. Table 5.2 summarizes possible responses.

Table 5.2   Responses to Attitude/Aptitude Challenges

Classification	Example	How to Respond
1. Willing and able	Good citizen	• Watch for burnout
	Control freak or martyr	• Monitor progress • Find additional support if needed • Provide individual coaching
2. Willing but unable	Positive incompetent (truly unable)	• Provide targeted training, coaching, and mentoring • Remove for damage control • Reassign to a doable task
	Person on leave (temporarily unable)	• Reassign responsibilities • Add short-term resources

Classification	Example	How to Respond
3. Unwilling but able	Thoughtful opponent (positive attitude but against proposed change)	• Use conflict management skills (cooperative negotiation and compromise)
	Negative obstructionist (negative attitude and against proposed change)	• Use conflict management skills (cooperative negotiation, then force, if necessary)
	Passive aggressor	• Create mechanisms to document and track implementation activities over time
4. Unwilling and unable	Hostile incompetent	• Remove for damage control • Reassign to a doable task

Source: © 2004 Jean A. King.

1. *The willing and able.* These are the people who get the job done, so needs assessors should assist them in their ongoing efforts. For overdoers who want to control every activity or who enjoy being organizational martyrs, it is important to monitor progress. If a person is truly becoming overwhelmed, relief should be available by providing additional resources or limiting the task. Individual coaching may help people focus on actions to move the plan forward efficiently or on how to best manage time for doing so. Watch for symptoms of burnout (emotional exhaustion, frequent illness, increased absenteeism, growing pessimism). If you observe these, consider reconfiguring roles and responsibilities before implementers become frustrated, get sick, or leave the organization.

2. *The willing but unable.* For the people who are truly unable to make the required changes, solutions include training to develop needed skills, one-on-one coaching to increase competence, or individual mentoring to improve performance. Removing or reassigning people to other tasks may become necessary if the change can't succeed with existing personnel. Altering responsibilities and adding short-term resources are

additional options. For example, when the executive director of a small not-for-profit organization needed chemotherapy that resulted in good days when she could work and bad ones when she had to stay home, the board hired a part-time manager to take over key functions for the 3 months that she underwent treatment.

3. *The unwilling but able.* Some people are able to do the work, but block change either by not buying in to the action plan or by intentionally setting out to sabotage it. Here, conflict management skills become useful (see Chapter 4). Positive people who don't buy in must have a way to express concerns and stay engaged constructively. Integrative negotiation to clarify disagreements and understandings can result in improved plans and an increased commitment to move forward. If consensus isn't possible, then compromise may lead to participation with goodwill. Obstructionists with sharply negative attitudes may require a more direct approach. Negotiation may make sense as a first step, but if obstructers are not interested in maintaining good working relationships, you may have to force compliance by firmly stating expectations as well as consequences for not complying, a risky move since a common response to forcing is withdrawal. Although the demands of various situations require different versions of conflict management, systematically identifying and addressing conflict can be a powerful way to keep action plans on track.

   Passive aggressors also can hold up implementation as others must wait for them to complete their part of the change effort. Postassessment plans must somehow provide accountability for promised actions by documenting implementation activities. One person may agree to become the monitor, noting what transpires at each meeting and then bringing up main points the next time the group convenes. An easily accessed and complete archive of carefully dated meeting minutes enables systematic tracking of progress. An action plan timetable (see Figure 2.7) makes decisions and next steps visible so that people may be held accountable for their tasks. Ignoring inaction or a lack of progress may demoralize those who are trying to implement change, thereby only making matters worse.

4. *The unwilling and unable.* The hostile incompetent presents a true challenge by being unwilling and unable to participate in

postassessment activities. How can a needs assessor work with people who not only have negative attitudes but who can't do the required tasks even if they wanted to? Facing up to these individuals is sobering, possibly necessitating their leaving the organization, but typically only after concerted and well-documented efforts for job improvement. Negative potential notwithstanding, *not* attending to these individuals puts any change effort at grave risk.

Regardless of how you analyze people's behaviors, using the dual concerns conflict strategies model in Chapter 4 (Figure 4.1), the individual attitude/aptitude matrix presented here (Table 5.1), or perhaps some other framework (such as personality or style preference inventories), the importance of attending to human detail during the change process cannot be overstated. People's opinions, feelings, and reactions matter. To ignore them is to risk a failed implementation.

❖ SUPPORTING PEOPLE DURING IMPLEMENTATION

The real question throughout postassessment is how to foster an environment where individuals can work effectively and enthusiastically on the action plan. Too often, such plans create stress for those who invest in change but find no break in their busy schedules for the new activities or additional work required. With that in mind, those in charge should consider how best to support individual efforts. Providing sufficient time, incentives or rewards, and evidence of change all help constructively sustain people through the implementation process.

Sufficient Time

Do people have sufficient time during the workday to engage in implementation activities? Change efforts often fail to provide the time needed to complete activities. Instead, tasks are added to busy workloads, and those who have an already full professional plate are suddenly asked to make time for things they hadn't counted on and for which they may not be prepared. Inequitable workloads can strain the implementation and ruin a needed and well-conceived change. Protecting people's time is a larger organizational issue that raises a number of considerations. What activities get dropped or postponed? What gets reassigned? Can change activities be integrated into routine workloads, or can some activities be eliminated or merged in the name of efficiency (or sanity)?

Incentives/Rewards

What incentives or rewards may encourage people to commit to change over time? For staff involved in implementing any action plan, this means "What's in it for me?" Incentives come before the fact, rewards afterward; while different things may work in different organizations, people typically appreciate special support for engaging in change efforts. Consider the following incentives for staff and participants during postassessment implementation.

Money

Paying people for additional work may make them feel better about the extra hours required for implementation. If available, such payment can take multiple forms (overtime, summer support, a salary increase, or a one-time bonus). A warning, though: Not everyone is interested in added responsibilities, compensated or not.

Time

For many, the gift of time makes a positive difference when feeling overwhelmed by a workload changed (often expanded) by the demands of an action plan. This may be especially true in organizations that have no money to support the implementation, regardless of its importance. Structuring routine meetings during the regular workday can allow people time to focus on the proposed change within their normal schedule.

Meaningful Work

For some people extra money or time is less important than the opportunity to do what they consider good work, especially if they support the action plan. People will devote extraordinary energy to meaningful initiatives. Such efforts may include welcoming professional discussion with peers, interactions with people considered interesting or powerful, or connecting with staff with whom they don't typically interact.

Respectful Treatment

This affective component of meaningful work is listed separately because treating people with respect—listening carefully to their issues and concerns, finding time for one-on-one consultations, and always ensuring that multiple voices are heard—can move an implementation forward. To not treat people well is to risk, during this critical phase, the failure of the entire needs assessment.

Food and Fun

This is not a joke. People often enjoy a party, so why not provide them something to eat and enjoyable interaction as postassessment activities unfold? Food and fun are listed last as they should clearly not be driving forces in any implementation, but creating creature comforts in social situations may improve people's interactions, fostering more relaxed conversation and an openness sometimes absent in meetings.

Evidence of Change

What evidence supports the fact that change is taking place? A true gardener can attest to the joy in observing a seedling's growth, from the first shoot breaking through the soil to the eventual flower that blooms. So, too, the implementation of an action plan. Documenting what is happening can confirm to those involved that changes are being made and identify areas that may need special attention. Picking the so-called "low-hanging fruit" (acting immediately on changes easily made) points to the possibilities of longer-term, institutionalized change. Evaluative processes that focus on the positive may prove highly appropriate in postassessment. Consider these examples: (a) Appreciative inquiry builds on what is working in an organization (Cooperrider & Whitney, 2005), (b) the success case method provides stories of people who are succeeding and those who are not (Brinkerhoff, 2003), and (c) the most significant change (MSC) technique encourages participants to tell stories about emergent outcomes (Davies & Dart, 2005). If seeing is believing, then evidence that something is really changing may help people stay the sometimes rocky course of the implementation. For example, when staff at a high school started working to change a competitive and negative culture, they asked the art teacher for high-quality student artwork that they then hung in the entry hallway. What had been a dark, cinder block first impression suddenly bloomed with color and creativity, signaling a change.

❖ ORGANIZATIONAL ISSUES THAT CHALLENGE CHANGE

Up to now, this chapter has focused on how individuals may deter postassessment progress and how to intervene to address such situations. Problems may involve interpersonal conflict or reveal individual attitude or aptitude characteristics, any of which may thwart implementation efforts. While these certainly present threats to change, they constitute only part of the implementation challenge. The other part deals with a broader set of concerns, where interventions previously described are insufficient because solutions require attention to organizational issues. While there may be overlap among individual, interpersonal, and organizational influences that require attention, needs assessors should consider the organizational contexts within which the eventual changes occur. Why? Because of the ever-changing nature of internal and external environments and their synergistic effects on people's interactions over time. Think about the following three settings:

- *The one-time needs assessment.* This common context consists of an assessment conducted once for a specific purpose, often in association with a funder's demands or expectations.
- *The periodic needs assessment.* If an organization is committed to meeting the needs of its stakeholders, it may periodically conduct an assessment to ensure that it is truly meeting the needs identified and to monitor changing needs over time.
- *Needs assessment for organizational learning.* This is an ongoing process over many years that involves, in a cycle of continuous improvement, collecting assessment data, developing and implementing an action plan, evaluating its outcomes, and then repeating the process. Ongoing needs assessment is one version of organizational learning that capitalizes on the experiential learning cycle (plan, act, reflect, revise)—the idea that organizations, like people, can improve their practices through knowledge and understanding that are shared among staff and lead to effective action.

Whatever the setting, needs assessors will have to establish conditions, structures, and system supports for success and respond to the unexpected. Keeping the bigger picture in mind throughout postassessment necessitates that all involved repeatedly ask what actions people can take to successfully facilitate the implementation. The role of needs assessors will vary whether they are internal or external to the organization. External needs assessors may not know the political situations likely to affect their work; internal needs assessors may require the support of influential leaders as people work to bring the action plan to life.

❖ ORCHESTRATING ORGANIZATIONAL CHANGE

The steps of postassessment move from action planning to action, always taking place within larger environmental contexts. Needs assessors should focus on these contexts (internal and external), structures in the organization to support the implementation, and resources necessary for the change process to succeed (Volkov & King, 2007). These topics, and how leaders constructively deal with them, are elaborated in numerous books on organization development and change (e.g., see Fullan, 2006, 2007, 2008; Kotter, 2007; Kotter & Cohen, 2002; Kouzes & Posner, 2007; Pfeffer & Sutton, 2000; Senge, 2006). Here we briefly discuss their relevance to implementing the needs assessment action plan.

Contexts

During postassessment the needs assessor must understand the external and internal organizational contexts, including decision-making processes, power hierarchies, and administrative culture. First determine if and to what extent the external environment is supportive of (or at least not opposed to) the proposed changes. In some cases funding agencies may encourage innovation by soliciting proposals to support such work. External stakeholders may be willing to provide support for the proposed changes, financially or through in-kind contributions.

The internal context requires similar attention to determine if and to what extent people inside the organization support (or again, at least do not oppose) the proposed changes. A positive, data-use-friendly internal context will support activities, which means it is important to understand the history of change in the organization. Have innovations come and gone over time? Are changes introduced quickly and never fully implemented before the organization moves on to the next? Have staff had bad experiences during earlier change efforts? Are they suffering from burnout for any reason? Key activities for the needs assessor here include

- ensuring that organizational leadership supports and shares responsibility for implementing the solution strategies,
- identifying and enlisting internal champions to lead the implementation, and
- focusing on early successes, relatively quick fixes (the "low-hanging fruit") that will demonstrate that the action plan really is going to work.

Structures

By purposefully creating or reinforcing certain structures within the organization, the needs assessor can facilitate the implementation of the action plan. Consider each of the following:

1. A critical first structure is a diverse and capable needs assessment oversight group, typically composed of members of the staff, the board of directors, and community members, who will initiate, advance, and ultimately evaluate the action plan implementation for the organization. The number of members and composition of the group will vary depending on the size of the organization but will not likely exceed 15. This group will be charged with affirming the steps of the action plan, reviewing data, monitoring the implementation, and proposing adjustments as needed. It will typically be led by the needs assessor, a leader from the needs assessment committee (NAC), or a key manager.

2. A second structure is a clear communication plan, including external public relations capability and internal transparency to relay needs assessment findings to stakeholders and to keep people in the loop over time about the ongoing implementation of the action plan. One important component of the plan is a formal, written document based on needs assessment data, which can be used to assess progress and propose adjustments as needed. The postassessment plan should have a timeline and benchmarks or checkpoints along the way, making progress visible for those participating, as well as an internal reporting/monitoring data tracking system. Incorporating a formal feedback mechanism in the decision-making process will ensure that what is proposed actually occurs or is modified based on new sets of circumstances.

3. The third structure is purposeful socialization into the implementation process. Needs assessors should never assume that people, whether longtime employees or new staff, will understand how the proposed changes relate to their work. Establishing clear expectations for people's roles and providing structured activities and sufficient time to make sense of required actions builds individual and organizational capacity to implement change. Tangible incentives may encourage participation, and the involvement of key leaders can foster the involvement of others. It is important to provide ample opportunities for reflection, including data-based discussions of successes, challenges, and failures in the organization as they relate to the proposed changes.

4. Closely related to socialization, peer learning mechanisms also facilitate implementation of the action plan. Creating ongoing learning activities through which people interact around the action plan content, whether through formal training, professional development, coaching, or informal opportunities for discussion, helps ensure that changes are understood and make sense to those who must act. Given the uncertainties that may emerge, it may be helpful to emphasize purposeful trust building (both between individuals and within the broader organization) and interdependent roles in the change process. It is important to allow adequate time and opportunities to collaborate, including, whenever possible, being physically together in an environment free from interruptions or socializing around implementation activities during the workday (collaboratively working on an action plan component during regular work hours, discussing needs assessment outcomes at brown-bag lunches, acknowledging/celebrating progress at afternoon or end-of-workday receptions).

Resources

Too often people pay to conduct a needs assessment without considering or providing resources to support its eventual outcomes in action. Postassessment demands that resources, financial and otherwise, be available for the ongoing implementation of the action plan. Absent these, people may experience the Rumpelstiltskin effect, asked to create the gold of change and improvement when all they see around them are piles of everyday, work-as-usual hay. The needs assessor, then, has the resource-related responsibility to identify and ideally expand access to resources for the implementation. Although it is unlikely that most needs assessors can dramatically affect the budget allocation process, they can ensure the availability of sufficient information on how to access existing resources (e.g., Web sites, professional organizations, and external consultants) and provide easy access to relevant research bases that contain best practices or evidence-based practice in the specific organizational content. They may even work with key staff members to propose long-term fiscal support (explicit, dedicated funding for implementing the action plan).

❖ RESPONDING TO THE UNEXPECTED

Mary Tyler Moore once quipped, "Worrying is a necessary part of life." For the needs assessor charged with implementing an action plan, worrying is not only necessary but essential. A strong implementation plan can launch a change effort, but it is inevitable that the unexpected will occur, often disrupting the best designs and intentions. Consider each of the following:

1. *Changes in the external environment.* These are from outside the organization and may include new mandates or legislative requirements, pressure from funders to engage in certain kinds of programs (e.g., research-based best practices), or the appointment or election of a key individual. Needs assessors should keep their metaphoric fingers in the wind and not become insulated from the larger context in which change is being implemented. In some cases external changes have the power to affect implementation dramatically, for better or worse. To ignore these big-picture forces puts the action plan at risk; quick response may keep actions on track.

2. *Internal personnel changes.* One of the challenges facing any change effort is what to do if key personnel leave. This is critical if the person who leaves has positional authority, is a charismatic idea champion, or is the driving force for the needs assessment and action plan. It can be equally difficult if there is routine turnover of staff members. For example, a particular social service agency, well known for both its high-quality practice and low salary schedule, loses roughly half its staff

each year, typically to better-paying organizations that value their experience. Such turnover creates a continuing challenge to making and sustaining meaningful change.

3. *Shifts in the budget.* Many organizations live in a continuous state of concern over funding, worrying about common "what if's." What if the price of heat and electricity continues to rise, the organization gets a major bequest, the levy doesn't pass, the roof suddenly needs major repair, the organization merges with another, or the application for the mammoth grant is successful? On the one hand, a sudden lack of resources can place postassessment in limbo as the staff struggles to address newfound budgetary constraints. On the other, a sudden infusion of resources is also problematic as this may raise expectations for immediate results despite the fact that it may be difficult to gear up quickly.

4. *Internal politics.* Even with positive intentions, competition and power have a way of emerging in organizations large and small. Chapter 4 pointed to the potential limiting effects of a competitive environment and goal structures. What power challenges may arise during the postassessment process? A needs assessor may be working in an organizational culture that doesn't value interaction or collaboration. There may be power spikes and surges as different people seek to assert authority or block changes they perceive as negative. There may be the chaos of an organization in crisis. Two things are clear. First, the organization's top leader can use his or her clout to support and move the action plan forward. The clout factor is powerful. When people see or hear a strong statement of support from that individual, they more substantially realize the importance of the implementation. Second, the clout factor is necessary but not sufficient. As Fullan's (1993) sixth lesson (Chapter 2) tells us, success requires support from both the top down (positional leader) and the bottom up (line staff and their leaders). The whole organization must come together around desired changes and work collaboratively to bring them to life.

5. *Miscommunication.* Even the best communication plan is only that—a plan. The potential for misunderstanding always exists, especially if the stakes for change are high. Sometimes cultural or language factors enter into the mix as diversity brings new perceptions, interpretations, or meanings. Rumors may surface

and, whether true or false, create their own energy in organizations. Keeping everyone in the loop is a major challenge as messages are sent and received in postassessment.

6. *Extended timelines.* A colleague of ours once noted that collaboration is a wonderful process until you actually want to get something done. It requires interaction and extended discussion. This may simply take more time than is available as the action plan moves forward. Time can become an issue as deadlines approach without the requisite action plan accomplishments.

Predicting and planning for these six types of events throughout the implementation process, turning the unexpected into the expected, may mark the difference between success and failure in implementing an action plan.

Highlights of the Chapter

This chapter addresses two challenges to implementing the needs assessment action plan. One is how to work with people as unique individuals who bring diverse attitudes and aptitudes to the change effort. The other is how to work with "big picture" challenges presented by the organization's internal and external contexts. We suggest the following to guide implementation effectively.

1. Use the "willing/able" matrix to identify and respond to individual characteristics that may block, frustrate, or obstruct implementation of an action plan (see Tables 5.1 and 5.2).

2. Invest in activities that support people during implementation, such as making time available, providing meaningful incentives, and documenting progress.

3. Examine the broader picture. Organizational contexts, structures, and resources influence change efforts. Leverage these for success whenever possible.

4. Expect the unexpected. Needs assessors forewarned and forearmed with potential solutions can respond more quickly to keep the action plan on track.

6

Evaluating the Entire Needs Assessment

Learning From the Expedition

Most successful change processes are invariably accompanied by strong, embedded evaluation and monitoring practices along the journey of change. For this reason it's important to consider evaluation at the outset rather than see it as just something to consider at the end.

—National College for School Leadership, 2009

❖ INTRODUCTION

The act of conducting a needs assessment presents multiple opportunities for evaluation—literally before, during, and after (in preassessment, needs assessment, and postassessment). To our minds, including components for evaluating both the implementation and its outcomes will strengthen every needs assessment and resulting action plan. Broadly speaking, evaluation is a systematic inquiry process that at its best provides people with high-quality information they can use in a variety of ways, including making decisions, improving their actions, judging their programs, or understanding what they've learned as a result. Evaluations "typically describe and assess what was intended . . . , what happened that was unintended, what was actually implemented, and what outcomes and results were achieved" (Patton, 2008, p. 5). Applying this idea to needs assessment means that every plan, from the beginning of the process to its conclusion, should include methods for collecting solid information that will answer people's questions as they work through the various phases. As stated in Chapter 3, for example, needs assessment plans should specify how progress will be monitored and evaluated so that, if necessary, changes can be made as the process moves forward.

Chapter 6 discusses how to evaluate the needs assessment itself. This differs from an evaluation of the resulting action plan, its implementation, and its outcomes. There are many resources available for those interested in learning about how to conduct such an evaluation; indeed, there is an entire field that works to understand how to do this. Our short list of recommendations for novices includes Davidson (2004); Fitzpatrick, Sanders, and Worthen (2004); O'Sullivan (2004); Patton (2008); and Russ-Eft and Preskill (2009).

Here we consider the benefits of evaluating the entire needs assessment and provide three overarching questions to guide that process: How are we doing? How did we do? What did we learn? For each, we present corresponding sets of probing questions to assist needs assessors in framing evaluation activities in their own contexts. We also list general methods for collecting evaluative information. Finally, we suggest the value of developing a brief plan for formative, summative, and reflective evaluation throughout the process.

❖ BUILD EVALUATION INTO
THE NEEDS ASSESSMENT PROCESS

Why is it important to build evaluation into the needs assessment process? Consider the following examples, and put yourself in the shoes of the needs assessors who found themselves in these situations.

- *Case 1.* Homeowners and longtime residents were genuinely excited to participate in the needs assessment process because many had specific ideas about how to reduce the acts of random violence that had plagued the community for years. Without thinking, the agency staff scheduled the focus group sessions during the day when most of the community members (who worked) were unable to attend. Several sessions had so few participants that the groups were canceled, and staff began to question people's commitment to express their concerns.

- *Case 2.* After months of hard work, the needs assessment report was finished, and the health department staff who had organized the assessment were ready to breathe a sigh of relief. They had met their deadline. Reviewing the focus group data from Somali mothers, they were surprised to see how few issues had been raised because they knew from their home visits the challenges these women faced. One staff member ran into a mother she knew well at a supermarket and explained her concern. "Oh," the woman said, "the interpreter spoke our language, but he told us not to say anything bad in case the program would be canceled."

- *Case 3.* Staff at the foundation were eager to respond to their new president's desire to base funding on current community needs, and the fact that an earlier needs assessment was over a decade old suggested it was high time to do another. But when they pulled the related files, they were dismayed to discover that the only document that remained from the first study was a dog-eared final report. No one who had participated in that process remained on staff, and no one had archived any of the plans and timelines, data collection instruments, debriefings on the process—nothing. The story of the earlier process had simply disappeared.

What do these examples mean? In the first case, the data collection plan was flawed and should have included evening hours. In the second, the mothers' data in all likelihood shouldn't have been included in the needs assessment since validity was questionable at best. In the third, the staff of the earlier assessment had failed to create an archive that would facilitate the work of future colleagues. Imagine different and more positive outcomes for a moment, all of which would have been possible if the needs assessment committees (NACs) had systematically included evaluation as an integral part of their ongoing activities. Hindsight may be 20/20, but there is nothing to do after the fact but acknowledge the flaws in a given assessment process. How much better it is to incorporate evaluation in all phases and use data to inform and improve activities.

Needs assessors must, however, keep in mind that for many people evaluation is distasteful. Some become anxious or even fearful, not knowing what to expect. This may be especially true of clients or program participants (which can impede obtaining information on Level 1 needs). Staff also may roll their eyes at yet another bureaucratic string tied to their funding (which reflects Level 2 needs). The prospect of time wasted on worthless tasks infuriates those who have had such experiences in the past. Thankfully, others have a different reaction and gravitate toward the positive potential of evaluation—the opportunity to collect information systematically about what's happening as their needs assessment occurs or what happens as a result of it and the chance to reflect on what they've learned. The key for needs assessors is to enhance the positive—the utility of evaluative information—while attending to the negative possibilities in gathering, writing, and discussing it. Focusing on the real questions of people who are in a position to use information, the primary intended users (Patton, 2008), increases the likelihood that evaluation will serve a real and valued purpose in the needs assessment, and that is worth serious consideration as the above cases suggest.

❖ OVERARCHING EVALUATION QUESTIONS

In thinking about the overall process of needs assessment, there are three overarching questions to ask, each of which relates to a specific time and set of evaluation activities and for each of which certain data collection methods make sense. These questions, the times typically associated with them, and the common evaluative labels for such inquiry are displayed in Table 6.1. As you further consider these questions and corresponding components, also remember the three levels of needs (clients, staff, and organization) and the importance of attending to each systematically.

Table 6.1 Summary of Overarching Questions

Question	Time in the Needs Assessment Process	Evaluative Terms
How are we doing?	During, throughout (preassessment, needs assessment, and postassessment)	Monitoring, formative
How did we do?	After, at the end (postassessment)	Summative
What did we learn?	Throughout, but especially at the end (preassessment, needs assessment, and postassessment)	Reflective

Source: © 1995 Jean A. King.

How Are We Doing?

Needs assessors and, once formed, the NAC can and should ask the first question appropriately from the initial meeting at the beginning of the study to final celebration of its completion. This encourages people to review the process as they go, actively evaluating as they move through various phases. Table 6.2 includes 10 sample probing questions that focus on different aspects of the needs assessment

Table 6.2 Questions for Evaluating a Needs Assessment as It Is Taking Place

Framing Question:	**How are we doing?**
Sample Probing Questions:	

1. Are you implementing the needs assessment as planned, or have you made changes?
2. If you've made changes, are they likely to affect the quality of the needs assessment?

(Continued)

Table 6.2 (Continued)

3. To what extent is the needs assessment adequately addressing the program context?

4. Are there any issues you have chosen not to address in the needs assessment? Why?

5. What can be done to enhance the participation of key individuals in the needs assessment?

6. Is there any resistance to the needs assessment process? If so, how are you addressing it?

7. Are people meeting deadlines, or does the timeline need to be revised?

8. Have there been problems in collecting data with the methods you have selected? If so, what can you do to improve the data collection?

9. Will you have sufficient amounts of high quality data to understand and document people's needs?

10. How are you keeping appropriate individuals apprised of the needs assessment process?

Source: © 1985 Jean A. King.

implementation. Such monitoring or formative evaluation may suggest changes that will strengthen the process, as demonstrated in the first case presented earlier. Given that information, the needs assessor could quickly add evening hours to ensure that working community members would be fairly included in the data collection.

A brief comment on terms is in order here. *Monitoring* is a term that comes from the world of government and large-scale international evaluations; it is often found in combination with the term *evaluation*—M&E, monitoring and evaluation—identifying it as the formative, shaping partner to a more judgmental evaluative conclusion. Similarly, many view the term *formative* as the partner of *summative,* where formative evaluations lead to programmatic improvements that result in an ultimate judgment about the program's value (Scriven, 1967).

What this means practically is that the responses to the "How are we doing?" question are plowed back as quickly as possible into improvements in the needs assessment to make sure the quality of the process will lead to usable information. To facilitate this, it may be helpful to make someone responsible for managing the "stuff" of the assessment—for example, dating key tables to monitor the process, taking action minutes that people actively review, and creating both hard-copy and electronic collections of all materials (meeting agendas and minutes, data collection instruments, data sets, etc.). Systematically including time in meetings for both informal, instantaneous reaction and more formal, thoughtful reflection will remind people to focus on what is working and what is not. As noted in Chapter 3, such discussions can actually enhance the needs assessment. What is technically called *process use* occurs when people involved in the assessment learn from the process itself (Patton, 2008). Asking leaders and staff to participate in conversations about the ongoing implementation may teach them about needs assessment as they reflect both individually and together about the actions being taken. In addition, needs assessors can ask people to complete simple evaluative surveys after meetings (see Figures 3.8a and 3.9a) or even send a more formal survey for midprocess reactions.

How Did We Do?

The second question is the companion to the first in that summative evaluation typically follows formative. In asking this question, needs assessors are engaged in a form of metaevaluation, evaluating the evaluative process. The extent and rigor of this metaevaluation will depend on the scope of the assessment and the time and resources available. Table 6.3 includes 10 sample probing questions that focus on the process and outcomes, intended and unintended, of the needs assessment planning and implementation. In the second case presented earlier, for example, the needs assessor faced a challenging decision about how to proceed: Use the mothers' data, knowing bias may be present, or find another way either to confirm the content or to

Table 6.3   Questions for Evaluating a Needs Assessment Once It Is Completed

Framing Question:	How did we do?
Sample Probing Questions:	
1. What parts of the needs assessment process went forward with little problem?	
2. What were the most difficult aspects of conducting the needs assessment? Did these affect the outcomes in any meaningful way?	

(Continued)

Table 6.3 (Continued)

3. How confident are you that the data collected are high quality and adequately document people's needs?

4. To what extent are the final needs assessment documents clearly written? Will key stakeholders be able to understand and apply the results?

5. Does the needs assessment action plan include specific action-oriented recommendations for specific people to act on?

6. Have you effectively engaged with the people who actually have to implement any changes proposed?

7. Does the action plan make sense in the existing context (e.g., financial, political)?

8. Are there any unintended outcomes or consequences, either good or bad, as a result of the needs assessment?

9. To what extent was the needs assessment cost-effective? Did you get your money's worth?

10. Have you created a complete record of the needs assessment process, including the changes made?

Source: © 1985 Jean A. King.

collect new data. How fortunate it is, however, to know of such bias rather than to proceed blindly using questionable data.

What this means practically is that once the plan and implementation are completed, the needs assessor should incorporate opportunities for a thoughtful discussion of their quality and any related implications for the final action plan. Minimally, this might mean bringing key participants together informally to discuss the process and its intended and unintended outcomes and then to problem solve any concerns or issues that arise that could affect the action plan's implementation. Individual or group interviews, including focus groups, could provide detailed, qualitative feedback on the process and results. Another idea would be to send a postassessment feedback survey, either paper or electronic, to all participants, compiling the information and using it to suggest possible revisions to the action plan. If there are questions about the effectiveness of the assessment as conducted, the needs assessor could hire an outside expert to review the process and its documents, performing a formal audit.

What Did We Learn?

The third question encourages people to think about what they know after the needs assessment experience that they did not know before. Ideally, it also establishes a written archive of these lessons for the organization. Table 6.4 includes 10 sample probing questions that focus on reflections, lessons learned, and preparation for a future assessment, however far in the future it might be.

Table 6.4 Questions for Learning From the Needs Assessment Process

Framing Question:	**What did we learn from the needs assessment process?**

Sample Probing Questions:

1. Have you kept adequate records to document both what you did and what was learned as a result of the needs assessment?
2. To what extent did your original plan require revision? Why?
3. Did you successfully respond to unexpected challenges during the needs assessment process?
4. Has the needs assessment increased the capacity of the organization to conduct other inquiries?
5. What did needs assessment participants learn as a result of participating?
6. How did your team change over the course of the needs assessment?
7. Are the lessons of the needs assessment applicable in other ways in the organization?
8. What parts of the process would you repeat during a future needs assessment? What would you do differently next time? Why?
9. If someone asked you to conduct another needs assessment, what steps would you be sure to take?
10. How will we know when it's time to do another needs assessment?

Source: © 2000 Jean A. King & Laurie Stevahn.

In creating an archive, the needs assessor is making the assumption that in a few years someone else will be asked to repeat the process and is creating a time capsule of all important documents and decisions related to the assessment. Giving one person the job of compilation increases the likelihood that at least that person will have all the necessary materials. These should be complete, accurate, and carefully labeled with dates and participants. Including templates will allow future needs assessors to start with what worked once, rather than with nothing. It is helpful to incorporate lessons learned from the needs assessment experience, reflections on what worked and what didn't, and what might be done differently the next time. Knowing the frequent fate of documents in any organization, having multiple copies in multiple forms—for example, at least one hard copy of everything in a notebook and an electronic version on a Web site that is also sent to every member of the needs assessment team—increases the likelihood that someone will have the information when it is next needed.

What this means practically is that in addition to ensuring that materials are archived, the needs assessor takes responsibility for creating opportunities for group discussion about what people have learned. Most people enjoy such reflections and are often surprised and pleased to see how the needs assessment process was an effective teacher. It sometimes makes sense to have a relatively small group craft a set of lessons learned and then ask other groups to revise them based on their experiences. In this way many people add ideas and experience a meaningful discussion.

❖ COLLECTING EVALUATIVE INFORMATION

Table 6.5 summarizes possible methods for collecting data on each of the three major questions, although a creative needs assessor may well make additions to the list.

Note that the facilitation procedures presented in Chapter 3 may also be used to carry out these suggested methods. Many of those procedures ask participants to provide information. Therefore, in addition to their postassessment purposes, these procedures can be used systematically to document processes and outcomes throughout all phases of assessment. Table 6.6 indicates which procedures are especially useful for formative, summative, or reflective purposes.

We find the procedures noted in the first column of Table 6.6 to be particularly useful for gathering formative needs assessment information. Some of these might routinely take place at regularly scheduled NAC meetings or periodically with staff and clients to determine how assessment decisions are affecting the larger organization. For

Table 6.5 Methods for Collecting Evaluative Information About the Needs Assessment

Framing Question	Methods for Collecting Information
How are we doing?	• Make one person responsible for compiling all materials related to the needs assessment, creating a record for periodic review • Hold routine reflection sessions (formal and informal) where people discuss specific details of the needs assessment implementation, what's going well, what the challenges are, and what might be changed to improve the process • Hand out simple feedback forms that are routinely completed by participants in needs assessment activities and then compiled and reviewed by the needs assessment team • Send a brief online survey to needs assessment participants at different points in the process to elicit their ideas about how things are going and what changes might be needed
How did we do?	• Hold informal debriefings with participants to critique the needs assessment process and outcomes • Conduct individual interviews with key members of the organization • Conduct focus group interviews with members of different groups who participated in the process • Send a postassessment feedback survey to all participants • Hire an outside expert to conduct a formal audit
What did we learn from the needs assessment process?	• Make one person responsible for compiling all materials related to the needs assessment and create an official archive for future efforts • Hold formal reflection sessions for people to frame the lessons learned from their participation in the needs assessment • Refine these lessons in a discussion with others who took part

Source: © 1995 Jean A. King.

Table 6.6   Facilitation Procedures for Evaluating/Documenting the Entire Needs Assessment

Procedures		*How are we doing?* Formative	*How did we do?* Summative	*What did we learn?* Reflective
1.	Voicing Variables	X		
2.	Voicing Viewpoints			
3.	Choosing Corners	X	X	
4.	Making Metaphors	X	X	
5.	Cooperative Interviews	X	X	X
6.	Roundtable/Roundrobin	X	X	X
7.	Check-In/Tune-In	X		
8.	Pluses/Wishes	X		
9.	PMI (Pluses/Minuses/Inquiries)/ PPP (Positives/Problems/Possibilities)	X	X	X
10.	Jigsaw			
11.	Graffiti/Carousel	X	X	X
12.	Concept Formation	X	X	X
13.	Concept Mapping/Mind Mapping			X
14.	Force Field Analysis	X	X	
15.	Fishbone Analysis	X		
16.	What? So What? Now What?	X		X
17.	Rubric Reflections	X	X	
18.	Fist to Five	X	X	
19.	Dot Voting	X	X	
20.	Bar Graphs	X	X	
21.	Cooperative Rank Order	X		
22.	Multi-Attribute Consensus Reaching (MACR)			
23.	Delphi Method/Nominal Group Technique			
24.	Constructive Controversy			

Source: © 2001 Laurie Stevahn & Jean A. King.

Note: See Chapter 3 for facilitation directions and sample materials.

example, needs assessors easily can facilitate *Procedure 8: Pluses/ Wishes* (see Figure 3.8) at every NAC meeting, summarize input, and thereby produce ongoing documentation. Similarly, organizational leaders may facilitate *Procedure 5: Cooperative Interviews* (see Figure 3.5) with various groups to get feedback on how well needs assessment structures and processes are working. We especially recommend such interviews before steering committees reconfigure or disband prior to transitioning to subsequent phases in the needs assessment model.

We also find the procedures noted in the second and third columns of Table 6.6 to be useful for summative and reflective evaluations, respectively. Several lend themselves to both purposes. For example, *Procedure 11: Graffiti/Carousel* (see Figure 3.11) can engage people in critiquing various components of the needs assessment at its completion (How did we do?) or in reflecting on wisdom gained from participating in needs assessment activities (What did we learn?). Sample topics (sentence starters) may include the following:

- The needs assessment committee worked best when . . .
- The needs assessment committee struggled most when . . .
- Phase II data collection worked well when . . .
- Phase II data collection was problematic when . . .
- Resources that especially helped during the needs assessment were . . .
- Resources we didn't have but needed during the needs assessment were . . .
- Phase III action planning worked well when . . .
- Phase III action planning was problematic when . . .
- I felt motivated to implement the action plan when . . .
- Implementing the action plan felt like a burden when . . .
- Communication in needs assessment worked best when . . .
- Communication in needs assessment was problematic when . . .
- I felt supported during the needs assessment when . . .
- I struggled with the needs assessment when . . .
- What I've learned from involvement in the needs assessment process is . . .
- Useful advice for those conducting future needs assessment studies ("do's" and "don'ts") includes . . .

Conversations on topics such as these (recorded, archived, and accessible for future use) contribute to the type of evaluation capacity building (e.g., see Compton, Baizerman, & Stockdill, 2002), process use (e.g., see Cousins, 2007; Patton, 2008), and systems learning (e.g., see Preskill & Torres, 1999; Senge, 2006) that underpin ongoing improvement in effective programs and organizations.

To determine how you will build formative, summative, and reflective evaluation into your needs assessment, we suggest you revisit the tables in this chapter as well as the facilitation directions in Chapter 3 and then select those ideas or procedures best suited to your circumstances. If you work in an organization where evaluations routinely take place, we anticipate that you will see many ways to elaborate the possibilities presented here. If, however, evaluation practice has not been the norm in your setting, we suggest starting small, building capacity as the assessment unfolds. We conclude this chapter by mapping how to feasibly evaluate an entire needs assessment from beginning to end.

❖ GETTING STARTED

At the onset, plan to evaluate the needs assessment as it is taking place (formative) and at its conclusion (summative), as well as documenting lessons learned (reflective). The Comprehensive Needs Assessment Evaluation Outline in Table 6.7 provides a basic map for integrating these three types of evaluation into the assessment before it begins. We have suggested two or three procedures for each box, but creative needs assessors will find ways to use others as well. As indicated, routinely obtain formative feedback at all NAC meetings throughout all phases of the assessment. This can easily occur at the end of every meeting by facilitating *Procedure 8: Pluses/Wishes*. Also plan to obtain both summative and reflective input from appropriate groups or stakeholders at the end of each phase, resources permitting. If resources are limited, conduct summative assessment and formalize lessons learned for the entire needs assessment at its conclusion (the end of Phase III). We suggest the checkbox strategies listed in Table 6.7 because of their feasibility. However, we also encourage adaptations or elaborations to address unique contexts, circumstances, and situations. Whether a needs assessor is highly experienced or new to evaluation practice, developing a one-page plan to evaluate the overall needs assessment before it begins helps needs assessors successfully accomplish the final steps of postassessment.

Table 6.7 Comprehensive Needs Assessment Evaluation Outline

Three-Phase Model	_Formative Evaluation_ How are we doing?	_Summative Evaluation_ How did we do?	_Reflective Evaluation_ What did we learn?
Phase I Preassessment	Collect input at every NAC meeting during this phase. Select a method best for your needs assessment situation (check one). □ Procedure 8: Pluses/Wishes □ Procedure 9: PMI/PPP □ Other _____	Collect input from the NAC, staff, clients, or other appropriate stakeholders on this phase at its end, resources permitting. Select a method best for your needs assessment situation (check one). □ Procedure 9: PMI/PPP □ Procedure 14: Force Field Analysis □ Procedure 17: Rubric Reflections □ Create your own survey □ Other _____	Collect input from the NAC, staff, clients, or other appropriate stakeholders on this phase at its end, resources permitting. Select a method best for your needs assessment situation (check one). □ Procedure 5: Cooperative Interviews □ Procedure 11: Graffiti/Carousel □ Other _____
Phase II Needs Assessment	Collect input at every NAC meeting during this phase. Select a method best for your needs assessment situation (check one).	Collect input from the NAC, staff, clients, or other appropriate stakeholders on this phase at its end, resources permitting. Select a	Collect input from the NAC, staff, clients, or other appropriate stakeholders on this phase at its end, resources permitting. Select a

(Continued)

147

Table 6.7 (Continued)

Three-Phase Model	Formative Evaluation *How are we doing?*	Summative Evaluation *How did we do?*	Reflective Evaluation *What did we learn?*
	▫ Procedure 8: Pluses/Wishes ▫ Procedure 9: PMI/PPP ▫ Other _____	method best for your needs assessment situation (check one). ▫ Procedure 9: PMI/PPP ▫ Procedure 14: Force Field Analysis ▫ Procedure 17: Rubric Reflections ▫ Create your own survey ▫ Other _____	method best for your needs assessment situation (check one). ▫ Procedure 5: Cooperative Interviews ▫ Procedure 11: Graffiti/Carousel ▫ Other _____
Phase III Postassessment	Collect input at every NAC meeting during this phase. Select a method best for your needs assessment situation (check one). ▫ Procedure 8: Pluses/Wishes ▫ Procedure 9: PMI/PPP ▫ Other _____	Collect input from the NAC, staff, clients, or other appropriate stakeholders on this phase at its end; or collect input on the entire needs assessment if not obtained previously. Select a method best for your needs assessment situation (check one). ▫ Procedure 9: PMI/PPP ▫ Procedure 14: Force Field Analysis ▫ Procedure 17: Rubric Reflections ▫ Create your own survey ▫ Other _____	Collect input from the NAC, staff, clients, or other appropriate stakeholders on this phase at its end; or collect input on the entire needs assessment if not obtained previously. Select a method best for your needs assessment situation (check one). ▫ Procedure 5: Cooperative Interviews ▫ Procedure 11: Graffiti/Carousel ▫ Other _____

Source: © 2004 Laurie Stevahn & Jean A. King.

Every needs assessment plan should identify methods for collecting evaluative information that will answer people's questions as they work through the three phases. This chapter outlines three types of evaluation that can address issues from beginning to end.

1. One type of evaluation asks needs assessors and the NAC to think about the needs assessment process as it is happening by asking, "How are we doing?"

2. A second type occurs after the needs assessment action plan is completed by asking, "How did we do?" Here people collect information about how the process went.

3. A third type involves reflection by asking, "What did we learn?" Here people document important lessons useful for conducting future needs assessment studies.

4. When evaluating a needs assessment, there are different methods for collecting data depending on the questions being asked, including reflection sessions, feedback forms, surveys, individual and group interviews, or even an outside audit.

5. Many of the facilitation procedures presented in Chapter 3 are useful for collecting, summarizing, and documenting the entire needs assessment.

6. Developing a one-page plan for formative, summative, and reflective evaluation throughout the needs assessment helps ensure that it actually will happen.

7. Creating an archive of materials from the needs assessment process and its outcomes enables organizations to build on prior experiences when conducting future endeavors.

Epilogue

Art and science have their meeting point in method.

—Edward Bulwer-Lytton
English Dramatist, Novelist, and Politician (1803–1873)

Most expeditions end by unpacking—suitcases and equipment literally; memories of people, places, events, and encounters figuratively. So, too, the end of postassessment. The entire needs assessment is evaluated; insights are discussed and documented as lessons learned; materials are organized and archived as useful tools for future projects. Over time, those who regularly conduct needs assessment studies or who guide data-driven decision-making projects in general develop tacit wisdom about their practice. In a sense, larger sets of learning emerge as practitioners reflect on a lifetime of travels.

Some experienced needs assessors will point to the importance of practicing frequently, reflecting on practice, fine-tuning skills, paying attention to change, and creating conditions in which it can flourish. Others will highlight the significance of relationships and interpersonal competence, sometimes overlooked in a field that tends to emphasize technical (rather than social) aspects of practice, such as design, data collection, analysis, and the like. Although sound methods do affect the credibility and usefulness of results in all studies, we would caution that effective methods applied in any of the needs assessment phases should never take the form of rigidly following checklists, directions, or instructions. Instead, skilled practitioners will artfully apply the science of needs assessment, fluently adapting to address the issues, circumstances, and situations in each unique context. As such, successful practice is more like fine craftsmanship, influenced by mastery of knowledge, frameworks, methods, and so on (the science that grounds practice) and by adept actions that address the complex nuances, personalities, customs, policies, and infrastructures, different in every setting (the art that enables effectiveness).

In our own professional and personal journeys that now span many years, we keep in mind our own short lists of principles for traveling and living. They have served us well and, interestingly, also recap much of what fills this volume, guidelines for getting the results of needs assessment used, for making meaningful change. In conclusion, we share these with you now.

❖ STEVAHN'S TIPS FOR TRAVELING

- *Pack light.* Never carry too much baggage; it will drag you down. You won't be able to change course quickly, take advantage of impromptu situations, or exercise flexibility in the face of new discoveries if you are overburdened with unnecessary trappings. In postassessment, this occurs when people spend too much time creating the perfect plan and devote too little energy early on enacting it. Instead, get on board and depart from the station (sooner rather than later) to uncover the virtues and shortcomings of your planned itinerary. Although targeting destinations and reserving transportation in advance is helpful, you cannot totally rely on such preset plans because they often shift en route. Do bring the basics (knowledge, skills, determination), but don't fill your suitcase with unnecessary items that will encumber progress (including dogged determination to follow your original plan; be prepared to revise it along the way).
- *Carry the right currency.* Context matters. Know and appreciate the environment, climate, and culture of your setting. Value is enhanced when people bring what they need for constructive interpersonal exchanges. This means being current in your knowledge of how transactions work as well as having the right denominations to engage in the process. Social exchanges are more productive when everyone speaks the same language, so learn the language spoken in context for respectful, meaningful, and constructive interaction.
- *Stay alert.* Keep your eyes open. Approach peaks and valleys in stride; both are likely to appear. Pinnacles will provide spectacular views, and pitfalls will demand detours—the wows and woes of travel. Pay attention to both because we learn from both. Problems almost always produce unimagined possibilities, often

for the better. So watch and use what you learn to deal with whatever comes your way.

- *Make friends.* Invest in relationships. You will go farther and have more fun in the company of others who, like you, will make unique contributions to plotting the path and reworking its course while on the road. Others will point to sites you would have missed, provide history helpful for navigation, and assist in solving issues that arise. Also, in the end, toasting success is sweeter when savored with others. It is meant to be participatory.

❖ KING'S RULES FOR LIVING

- *Never panic.* On the one hand, needs assessment work is extremely important, improving lives of clients, enhancing the capabilities of program providers, and strengthening the effectiveness of organizations. On the other hand, it is rare that someone dies as the result of some aspect of the needs assessment process. Keep a healthy perspective throughout. Whatever you face, collaboratively forge ahead, drawing upon the singular talents, skills, and perspectives that every individual can contribute toward creatively meeting the challenge.
- *Solve the problem.* Problems become friends because we learn from tackling them. In fact, success requires struggling with difficulties, anticipated or not, that seem to frustrate progress, so don't avoid them. Instead, view problems as opportunities and confront each with a can-do attitude. Here, an old and saccharine adage is instructive: When life gives you lemons, make lemonade. But remember people must take hold of the lemons, squeeze them vigorously, add water and sugar, and stir to achieve desired results. The same is true in needs assessment; creatively transforming a calamity into an innovative solution requires everyone's effort.
- *Keep the big picture in mind.* Although attention to detail at times is critical to achieving goals, never let single trees block your view of the entire forest. The big picture brings the overall vision or mission to bear on the particular activities of people engaged in their daily work. In fact, keeping people focused on a larger valued purpose actually becomes a compelling part of what motivates change. It's not that details don't count, because they do, but focusing on particulars can become unproductive

to the overall effort, noted previously, as when people devote too much time and energy to developing a plan and not enough to carrying it out. Similarly, avoid micromanaging people's work, which tends to stifle the creativity, innovation, and passion upon which change efforts thrive.

- *Be nice.* Again, relationships matter. We can't emphasize this enough. It is through constructive relationships that the work of postassessment is accomplished. Always listen, respect differences, convey understanding, disagree in agreeable ways, engage in mutual problem solving, and try to seek outcomes that benefit everyone. Continuously strive to nurture cooperative conditions that will support everyone's efforts throughout the needs assessment journey. Organizational change most fundamentally is about people coming together to get the job done, so keep those with whom you work close to heart. By focusing on relationships, Phase III can lead to the meaningful change that is the needs assessment's ultimate goal.

References

Altschuld, J. W., & Kumar, D. D. (2009). *Needs assessment: An overview.* Thousand Oaks, CA: Sage.

Altschuld, J. W., & Witkin, B. R. (1999). *From needs assessment to action: Transforming needs into solution strategies.* Thousand Oaks, CA: Sage.

Belasco, J. A. (1990). *Teaching the elephant to dance: Empowering change in your organization.* New York: Crown Publishers.

Bennett, B., & Rolheiser, C. (2001). *Beyond Monet: The artful science of instructional integration.* Toronto, ON: Bookation.

Bolman, L. G., & Deal, T. E. (2001). *Leading with soul: An uncommon journey of spirit* (2nd ed.). San Francisco: Jossey-Bass.

Bolman, L. G., & Deal, T. E. (2008). *Reframing organizations: Artistry, choice, and leadership* (4th ed.). San Francisco: Jossey-Bass.

Brett, J. M. (2007). *Negotiating globally: How to negotiate deals, resolve disputes, and make decisions across cultural boundaries* (2nd ed.). San Francisco: Jossey-Bass.

Brinkerhoff, R. O. (2003). *The success case method: Find out quickly what's working and what's not.* San Francisco: Berrett-Koehler.

Compton, D. W., Baizerman, M., & Stockdill, S. H. (Eds.). (2002). The art, craft, and science of evaluation capacity building. *New Directions for Evaluation, 93.*

Cooperrider, D. L., & Whitney, D. (2005). *Appreciative inquiry: A positive revolution in change.* San Francisco: Berrett-Koehler.

Cousins, J. B. (Ed.). (2007). Process use in theory, research, and practice. *New Directions for Evaluation, 116.*

Davidson, E. J. (2004). *Evaluation methodology basics: The nuts and bolts of sound evaluation.* Thousand Oaks, CA: Sage.

Davies, R., & Dart, J. (2005). *The "most significant change" (MSC) technique: A guide to its use.* Retrieved February 14, 2009, from http://www.mande.co.uk/MSCGuide.htm

Deutsch, M. (1949a). A theory of cooperation and competition. *Human Relations, 2,* 129–151.

Deutsch, M. (1949b). An experimental study of the effects of cooperation and competition upon group process. *Human Relations, 2,* 199–231.

Deutsch, M. (1973). *The resolution of conflict: Constructive and destructive processes.* New Haven, CT: Yale University Press.

Deutsch, M. (2006). Cooperation and competition. In M. Deutsch, P. T. Coleman, & E. C. Marcus (Eds.), *The handbook of conflict resolution: Theory and practice* (2nd ed., pp. 23–42). San Francisco: Jossey-Bass.

Fisher, R., Ury, W., & Patton, B. (1991). *Getting to yes: Negotiating agreement without giving in* (2nd ed.). New York: Penguin Books.

Fitzpatrick, J. L., Sanders, J. R., & Worthen, B. R. (2004). *Program evaluation: Alternative approaches and practical guidelines* (3rd ed.). New York: Pearson Education.

Fullan, M. (1993). *Change forces: Probing the depths of educational reform*. London: RoutledgeFalmer.

Fullan, M. (1999). *Change forces: The sequel*. London: RoutledgeFalmer.

Fullan, M. (2003). *Change forces with a vengeance*. London: RoutledgeFalmer.

Fullan, M. (2006). *Turnaround leadership*. San Francisco: Jossey-Bass.

Fullan, M. (2007). *The new meaning of educational change* (4th ed.). New York: Teachers College Press.

Fullan, M. (2008). *The six secrets of change: What the best leaders do to help their organizations survive and thrive*. San Francisco: Jossey-Bass.

Johnson, D. W. (1967). The use of role reversal in intergroup competition. *Journal of Personality and Social Psychology, 7*, 135–141.

Johnson, D. W. (1997). *Reaching out: Interpersonal effectiveness and self-actualization* (6th ed.). Boston: Pearson Education Allyn & Bacon.

Johnson, D. W., & Johnson, F. P. (2009). *Joining together: Group theory and group skills* (10th ed.). Boston: Pearson Education Allyn & Bacon.

Johnson, D. W., & Johnson, R. T. (1989). *Cooperation and competition: Theory and research*. Edina, MN: Interaction Book Company.

Johnson, D. W., & Johnson, R. T. (2005a). New developments in social interdependence theory. *Genetic, Social, and General Psychology Monographs, 131*(4), 285–358.

Johnson, D. W., & Johnson, R. T. (2005b). *Teaching students to be peacemakers* (4th ed.). Edina, MN: Interaction Book Company.

Johnson, D. W., & Johnson, R. T. (2007). *Creative controversy: Intellectual challenge in the classroom* (4th ed.). Edina, MN: Interaction Book Company.

Johnson, D. W., & Johnson, R. T. (2009). An educational psychology success story: Social interdependence theory and cooperative learning. *Educational Researcher, 38*(5), 365–379.

Joyce, B., Weil, M., & Calhoun, E. (2009). *Models of teaching* (8th ed.). Boston: Pearson Education Allyn & Bacon.

Kotter, J. (2007). Leading change. *Harvard Business Review, 85*(1), 96–103.

Kotter, J., & Cohen, D. A. (2002). *The heart of change: Real-life stories of how people change their organizations*. Boston: Harvard Business School Press.

Kouzes, J. M., & Posner, B. Z. (2007). *The leadership challenge* (4th ed.). San Francisco: Jossey-Bass.

Lewicki, R. J., Saunders, D. M., & Barry, B. (2010). *Negotiation* (6th ed.). Boston: McGraw-Hill.

Marcus, E. C. (2006). Change and conflict: Motivation, resistance, and commitment. In M. Deutsch, P. T. Coleman, & E. C. Marcus (Eds.), *The handbook of conflict resolution: Theory and practice* (2nd ed., pp. 436–454). San Francisco: Jossey-Bass.

National College for School Leadership. (2009). *Evaluating and monitoring change—has it made a difference?* Retrieved August 10, 2009, from http://www.ncsl.org.uk/modelsofleadership-index/modelsofleadership-resources-index/modelsofleadership-resources-actionplanning/modelsofleadership-resources-evaluating.htm

O'Sullivan, R. (2004). *Practicing evaluation: A collaborative approach.* Thousand Oaks, CA: Sage.

Pascale, R., Millemann, M., & Gioja, L. (2000). *Surfing the edge of chaos.* New York: Crown Business Publishing.

Patton, M. Q. (2008). *Utilization-focused evaluation* (4th ed.). Thousand Oaks, CA: Sage.

Pfeffer, J. (2007). *What were they thinking? Unconventional wisdom about management.* Boston: Harvard Business School Press.

Pfeffer, J., & Sutton, R. I. (2000). *The knowing-doing gap: How smart companies turn knowledge into action.* Boston: Harvard Business School Press.

Preskill, H., & Torres, R. T. (1999). *Evaluative inquiry for learning in organizations.* Thousand Oaks, CA: Sage.

Pruitt, D. G., & Carnevale, P. J. (1993). *Negotiation in social conflict.* Pacific Grove, CA: Brooks/Cole.

Reeves, D. B. (2006). *The learning leader: How to focus school improvement for better results.* Alexandria, VA: Association for Supervision and Curriculum Development.

Reeves, D. B. (2009). *Leading change in your school: How to conquer myths, build commitment, and get results.* Alexandria, VA: Association for Supervision and Curriculum Development.

Russ-Eft, D., & Preskill, H. (2009). *Evaluation in organizations: A systematic approach to enhancing learning, performance, and change* (2nd ed.). Cambridge, MA: Perseus Publishing.

Scriven, M. (1967). The methodology of evaluation. In R. Tyler, R. Gagné, & M. Scriven (Eds.), *AERA monograph series on curriculum evaluation, 1* (pp. 39–83). Chicago: Rand McNally.

Senge, P. M. (2006). *The fifth discipline: The art and practice of the learning organization* (Rev. ed.). New York: Doubleday.

Stacey, R. (1992). *Managing the unknowable: Strategic boundaries between order and chaos in organizations.* San Francisco: Jossey-Bass.

Stacey, R. (1996). *Complexity and creativity in organizations.* San Francisco: Berrett-Koehler.

Stacey, R. (2007). *Strategic management and organisational dynamics: The challenge of complexity* (5th ed.). London: Pearson Financial Times Press.

Stevahn, L., & King, J. A. (2005). Managing conflict constructively in program evaluation. *Evaluation, 11*(4), 415–427.

Stevahn, L., King, J. A., Ghere, G., & Minnema, J. (2005). Establishing essential competencies for program evaluators. *American Journal of Evaluation, 26*(1), 43–59.

Tuckman, B. (1965). Developmental sequence in small groups. *Psychological Bulletin, 63,* 384–399.

Tuckman, B., & Jensen, M. (1977). Stages of small group development revisited. *Group and Organizational Studies, 2,* 419–427.

Volkov, B., & King, J. A. (2007). *A checklist for building organizational evaluation capacity.* Retrieved July 25, 2009, from http://www.wmich.edu/evalctr/checklists/ecb.pdf

Wheatley, M. (2005). *Finding our way: Leadership for an uncertain time.* San Francisco: Berrett-Koehler.

Index